Congratulations!

5/1/83

Dear Julie,

This is for you to have
at hand, for those times
when graff is "Vic Mature'
and laughing is the best cure —
I hope you have
A laughter and smiles
all of us deserve
Thanks for being such
a great friend — I love
you're special — I love
you —

Alexandra

# MAN BITES MAN
## *TWO DECADES OF SATIRIC ART*
*Edited by* Steven Heller

# MAN BITES MAN

## TWO DECADES
## OF DRAWINGS AND CARTOONS
## BY 22 COMIC AND SATIRIC ARTISTS

1960 *to* 1980

R.O. BLECHMAN
George BOOTH
Jean-Pierre DESCLOZEAUX
Jules FEIFFER
Paul FLORA
André FRANÇOIS
Edward GORĒY
Edward KOREN
Pierre LE-TAN
David LEVINE
Bill LEE

Eugene MIHAESCO
Lou MYERS
Robert OSBORN
Hans Georg RAUCH
Arnold ROTH
Ronald SEARLE
Jean-Jacques SEMPÉ
Edward SOREL
Ralph STEADMAN
Tomi UNGERER
Gahan WILSON

## *Edited by* Steven Heller

### Foreword *by* TOM WOLFE

*Design Assistance by* TONY HO

A & W Publishers, *New York*

Published by
A & W Publishers, Inc.
95 Madison Avenue
New York, New York 10016

Library of Congress Catalog Card Number: 81-66212
ISBN: 0-89479-086-2

Printed in United States of America

# DEDICATION

This Book is dedicated to three
giants of the comic arts

Art Young
Gluyas Williams
and
Otto Soglow

# FOREWORD
*by TOM WOLFE*

I can't think of anyone—even among the artists themselves—who has done more for contemporary American satiric art than our impresario for this volume, Steven Heller. Heller is like one of those legendary ice wall mountain climbing team captains: an avalanche has swept the whole party into a bottomless crevasse, and now, out of food, freezing, bereft of hope, everyone longs only for the sleep that will end the agony forever, but the captain will have none of it and methodically makes them jiggle their limbs and clap their Insuliner gloves together and prop their eyes open and keep talking, so as to prevent the final cryogenic coma from enveloping them...until...until...

In the case of Heller and his life support system for American caricaturists and illustrators, it is too early to tell how the drama will come out. After all, satiric art has been in a state of decline all over the West for fifty years now. The reasons have been obvious enough. Paramount has been the fall from fashion—plunge is more like it—of realistic painting. It was not by chance that the great century of caricature, 1820-1920, was also the great century of "literary" or vignette painting. All artists were expected to be expert in the rendering of face, figure, gesture, costume, landscape, architecture, and interiors; which is to say the technical essentials of caricature, a form demanding, above all else, *l'image juste.* Figure and still life continue to be taught in most art schools, but they are regarded as incidental to the development of the artist and, indeed, have meant nothing in the careers of the most highly praised American artists of the past twenty-five years. The same can be said for caricature's intellectual essentials: wit, political sophistication, a sense of history, and an appetite for the Vanity Fair. Today in the art schools the prevailing assumption is that such things are worse than useless. They are impediments, since an artist should be a *holy beast,* receiving impulses straight from the godhead without the screen of analysis. When young artists are encouraged to be intellectual slovens, like actors or dancers, they are happy to oblige.

Meanwhile, developments outside the art world have worsened the situation in an all too ironic fashion. The past half-century has seen a softening of the sanctions against libel and sedition in most Western countries. The day when a Daumier or a Thomas Theodor Heine could go to jail for ridiculing a head of state is over. Today a caricaturist can spend ten years attacking the high and the mighty in America—and the worst that can happen to him is that he will be summoned to the White House for a white-tie-and-decorations Salute to the Arts banquet, and the best is that one time out of a hundred the victim of his venomous brilliance will not call up the next day in a hearty voice asking if he can please buy the original. Which is to say, democracy, tolerance, and easy times have removed much of the danger and the *joie de combat* from caricature.

None of this dismays Steve Heller, however. He has set himself a goal: "I hope to find and inspire as many intelligent draftsmen and thinkers as possible before the field of graphic humor is totally consumed by the gag cartoon and television." I am amazed at the number of projects he has orchestrated toward that end in the dozen years since he started work, at eighteen, as art director of the *New York Free Press.* He has staged two important exhibitions of the olympians of satiric art—Heine, Paul, Thuny, and other artists who worked for the German humor magazine *Simplicissimus* in the first quarter of this century—and he is currently assembling a show of their French counterparts, the artists of L'Assiette au Beurre. In 1980, he organized a show of American political caricature of the 1970s, at the American Institute of Graphic Arts. He has edited three marvelously eccentric books of illustrations, *Artists' Christmas Cards, The Book of Waters, The Empire State Building Book,* and *Sin City Fables* (with Steven Guarnaccia, Alfa Betty-Olsen, and Marshall Efron), and is at work on *The Racist Image: Ethnic and Racial Stereotypes in Popular American Art.* He also serves on the advisory panel of the Swann Foundation for Caricature and Cartoons. All of this has been in addition to his work as an art director for many newspapers, magazines, and publishing houses, and, from time to time, as an illustrator himself. He is currently art director of the *New York Times Book Review.*

I should mention that Heller has only just turned thirty. If youth, intelligence, and monomania can save the day, then I say there is hope.

# ACKNOWLEDGEMENTS

This page is devoted to the many people who aided in the preparation of this book.

Many thanks to: Larry Alexander, my publisher, without whom this project would never have happened. Ruth Pollack, my editor, whose enthusiasm and support made working with A&W Publishers a pleasure. Cindy Lake, whose technical expertise was invaluable (thanks for the extra color!). Angela Miller, who made it possible for me to work with A&W in the first place. And Sarah Jane Freyman, my agent and very good friend.

Many of the artists in *Man Bites Man* are represented by John Locke (Searle, Francois, Desclozeaux, Gorey, and Rauch) and Ted Riley (Le-Tan, Koren, and Sempé)—two of the most sensitive art agents I have had the pleasure to work with. Without their help the compilation of this book would have been twice as difficult. Thanks to Milton Newborn (who represents Roth and Sorel) for allowing me to rummage through his files. Thanks to the Forum Gallery for guiding me through David Levine's collected works. My expressed gratitude goes to Edward Spiro, who schlepped all over town in order to photograph many of the larger pieces in this book. Tony Ho assisted me in the layout and design. Al Hawkins, Nestor Delgado, Paul Hacker, and Ed Gross offered much needed assistance.

Various publishers allowed me to reproduce drawings from previously published collections (a selected bibliography can be found on page 222). Thanks to: Michelle Urry at *Playboy;* Ray Shapiro at the *New York Review of Books;* Joyce Engelson at Richard Marek, Inc.; Bea Hurowitz at Simon & Schuster; Peter Workman and Chris Powers at Workman Publishing; Jill Frisch at *The New Yorker;* Robert Putz, president of Argos Verlag (West Germany). Very special thanks go to Daniel Keel, Anne Elizabeth Suter, and Odette A. Brandli at Diogenes Verlag (Zurich). I am most grateful for their help in supplying me with books, addresses, and negatives. (A bibliography of Diogenes cartoon books appears on page 224). Thanks also to Lyla Karpf at the Jay Action Agency; Penthouse International, Albin Michel (Paris); Denoel (Paris); the *New York Times,* the *Village Voice, Audubon Magazine; Holiday; Town and Country; Travel and Leisure; Politiks; Punch; Esquire;* and Rowhalt Verlag (West Germany).

It goes without saying that all the artists involved with this project have given of their time generously; thanks to them for selecting material, calling on the phone, answering letters, and putting up with all my queries. I would especially like to thank Ed Koren, whose enthusiastic response when I first told him about this book gave me the courage to continue; Ronald Searle for his continued support; Bill Lee for helping with the title; and Jules Feiffer for inviting me to work on another exciting project. Thanks to Tom Wolfe for his involvement with this and other endeavors. I am grateful to Sheila Wolfe at *Harper's* magazine for being such a "booster." Thanks, also, to Walter Herdeg, editor and publisher of *Graphis,* for giving me the opportunity to write about many of my favorite artists.

I regret that because of space, that many artists whom I admire are not included in this volume: TIM, Roland Topor, Gerald Scarfe, Al Hirschfeld, Lee Lorenz, Roger Law, Robert Grossman, Brad Holland, and Randall Enos. I hope that in another compilation I will be able to rectify some of these omissions.

Many friends have helped to expand my knowledge and appreciation of the comic arts: Fritz Eichenberg has been a close friend and teacher; Brad Holland introduced me to the legacy of German satiric art, now my foremost passion. Art Spiegelman opened up the world (and language) of the comic strip; Ralph Shikes, a valuable new friend, authored *The Indignant Eye,* the most insightful book on this subject; Bernard Riley, curator of Applied Graphic Arts at the Library of Congress, has generously given of his time, allowing me to pore through the countless boxes of original and printed matter in the Cabinet of Illustration; Draper Hill and Ed Sorel have added to my knowledge of caricature; Frank McCabe has supplied me with wonderful old magazines; the Paegant Bookstore in New York, the Starr Bookstore in Boston, and Lord Randall's in Marshfield, Massachusetts, have supplied me with important antiquarian and out-of-print cartoon collections. Thanks, also, to Dr. James Fraser at Fairleigh Dickenson University's Friendship Library and Arthur Cohen at Ex-Libris for affording me the opportunity to study important comic journals.

The following friends and acquaintances, whether they know it or not, helped in making this book a reality: My parents, Steve Schwartz, Sel Lederman, Lucie Binger, Marty Fox, Andy Kner, Mike Valenti, Mary Frank, Richard Yeend, Jasmine Katz, Caroline Hightower, Deborah Trainer, Nathan Gluck, Walton Rawls, Antonia Eichenberg, Harvey Shapiro, Richard Locke, Arthur Gelb, Marshal Arisman, Claudia Desclozeaux, Kathinka Ditterich, Bob Eisner, and Gary Cosimini. Thanks to Alan Fern for inviting me to become a member of the Swann Foundation for Caricature and Comic Art. And special thanks to Louis Silverstein for giving me the opportunity to work at the *New York Times.*

And, most of all, thanks and love to Julia Goggin, my wife, for putting up with my madness.

# INTRODUCTION

*by STEVEN HELLER*

*Several [philosophers] have defined man as "an animal which laughs." They
might equally well have defined him as an animal which is laughed at.*

—Henri Bergson
*Laughter: An Essay on the Meaning of the Comic*

When I was first asked to compile a book of cartoons, I balked at the thought of yet another cartoon anthology. Every few years we are treated to an album that purports to contain the best work of a specific time. What we find instead are a number of gag-styled cartoons once rejected by *The New Yorker* and subsequently revived by an editor who separates the wheat from the chaff and keeps the chaff. Usually the cartoons are printed on rag bond with ink so gray that the book can only be seen under a strong light. I have always thought that collections of this kind ultimately trivialize all graphic humor. And so, in order to promote a better appreciation for its diversity, I have compiled *Man Bites Man,* which presents portfolios of work by twenty-two contemporary graphic satirists, cartoonists, caricaturists, storytellers, and commentators, all with markedly different styles and points of view, all exemplars of the political, social, and cultural relevance of this art.

\*     \*     \*

Visual humor is manifest in a variety of forms: the political cartoon, the gag cartoon, the comic strip, the comic print, the animated cartoon, caricature, illustration, and sculpture (all but film, sculpture, and the "daily" editorial cartoon are represented in this book). The work of each artist here reflects personal motivations and influences, including political and aesthetic concerns. Graphic satire is variously used as a weapon against hypocrisy, as a devise for describing the human condition, and a means of entertainment. Drawing style—the artist's trademark —runs the gamut from economical sketchy lines to harsh broad brushstrokes, from mannered elegance to misproportioned grotesquery. The common thread that binds these artists together is their need to communicate *ideas.* Although humor is essentially the vehicle for this exchange, the resultant drawings are not always funny. What differentiates the cartoons in this collection from burlesque (or slapstick) gag is basically a respect for the viewer. Inherent in the work here is a passion for the absurd and the ability to subtly articulate the irony of the human condition. Tired clichés are rejected in favor of a personal visual vocabulary.

We are told by art pundits that drawings—virtually all drawings—are inconsequential compared with "more significant" paintings or sculpture, and that cartoons (originally a term used to describe a study or preparatory sketch for a painting), being topical by nature, are irrelevant to the history of art. This fallacy has been perpetrated for too long. Many important satiric drawings make broader, more viable statements by speaking to societal issues in aesthetic as well as humanist terms. A number of the drawings in *Man Bites Man* evidence this quality.

Historically, graphic humor served different needs. Before television and other electronic media dulled our visual senses, satiric drawings helped the average citizen bring into focus the issues of national or international importance. The satiric journal and the comic weekly were the most influential media of the nineteenth century, in as much as the journal format informed its audiences with a regular diet of comic drawings that assaulted social, governmental, and religious foibles. Daumier's lithographs were among many that exposed, through insightful humor, the corruption of his time while they imparted images of timeless relevance. His inflammatory characterizations of lawyers, judges, teachers, and doctors continue to have the ring of truth.

\*     \*     \*

Satiric representations date back to the ancient Egyptians, specifically in anthropomorphic depictions that were printed on papyrus. Early graphic political commentary has been excavated at Pompeii in the form of etchings on stone columns (this is, in fact, the origin of the term *graffiti*). The Greek spirit of parody was applied to even the most sacred mythology. People of the medieval world were great admirers of animals, and so symbolically domesticated them by depicting their peculiarities as a means of commenting on mankind. Artists of the Middle Ages borrowed grotesque imagery from antiquity to characterize all manner of life. For instance, gargoyles were used to comically describe the sins of greed, gluttony, and avarice.

Court fools and minstrels were the original satiric commentators appearing in living cartoons that lampooned their audience. Their actions and dress later affected modes of graphic representation (much in the same manner that Charlie Chaplin's comedic style has influenced dozens of contemporary comic artists).

*Caricature* was the term used to refer to all graphic forms of satiric and burlesque comedy of the past three centuries (the word *cartoon* was originally applied to humorous drawing in 1841 and then not commonly used until the end of the century). The theory of *caricatura*—the search for the perfect distortion —as practiced by Annibale Carracci during the late sixteenth century was a rebellion against the established definition of beauty (more an aesthetic problem than a satiric tool). Time had to pass before caricatured distortion was employed as a humorous device. In order for satire to flourish, certain prerequisites were necessary—not the least of which was societal stability. (It is true today that a free society is more apt to encourage comic criticism as a means of ventilating frustration.) It was after the English Restoration of the seventeenth century, which marked the end of Cromwell's puritanical reign, when satiric prints became more widespread. Until then, playing cards, produced in limited numbers and primarily for the upper class, were the principal vehicle for lampooning parliamentary leaders. A revival of *liberal law* in Britain eventually created and nourished the climate in which Jonathan Swift wrote his profound satires and Hogarth popularized his moral comedies.

Printing technology played an important role in the development of graphic comedy. In 1796, the discovery of lithography by Alois Senefelder revolutionized the production and the form of the art. The lithographic process not only offered a speedier means to create images—the artist could draw directly on the litho stone, rather than rely on the dubious talents of an engraver to replicate his drawing—but it also was less expensive to produce a greater quantity of prints and the savings were passed on to the consumer, of course. This encouraged the growth and distribution of newspapers and periodicals.

The French satirists benefited most from this German discovery. Having experienced a revolution of major proportions and then a return to monarchy, nineteenth-century France was a society fraught with turmoil. The prevailing mass sentiment of the 1830s was republican, and the bourgeois king was viewed with contempt, especially by the caricaturists. In contrast to Britain at the time, where certain freedoms were afforded the comic artist, the insecure Louis Philippe enforced harsh censorship decrees that forbade artists to ridicule either his office or his court. Charles Philipon—satirist, entrepreneur, and founder of *La Caricature* and *La Charivari* (the foremost political newspapers in France and home of Daumier, Grandville, Travies and Gavarni)—was jailed for his acid satires against the king. Ultimately, however, these restrictions had a positive effect on all caricature. Without the royal target of ridicule, it was incumbent on the artists to attack the enemy from the back door. The powerful satires of the era that commented on society, the military and the church will always be remembered by students of caricature.

Comic art in Britain during the late eighteenth and early nineteenth centuries was dominated by James Gillray, Thomas Rowlandson (both inspired by Hogarth), and, later, George Cruikshank defined a particular mode of humor. All created comic prints—engravings and etchings primarily purchased by the middle class—which alternately attacked the enemies of England and lampooned the class structure at home. In 1841 *Punch: The London Charivari* was founded and soon became the single most important outlet for humor of the next half-century. (It was in an early issue of the magazine that the term *cartoon* was afforded new meaning.) A handful of masterful draftsmen, including William Makepeace Thackeray, John Leech, George Du Maurier, John Tenniel, Charles Keene, Richard Doyle (and decades later, H.R. Bateman) sat at the "Mahogany Tree," developing their graphic wit and wisdom. Since the contributors were basically at ease with their monarchy and constitutional government, their political barbs were duller than their French counterparts. These satirists addressed themselves primarily to society, its manners and morals, as well as some vicious attacks on the papacy and various world leaders (Abe Lincoln was a favorite target during the Civil War years). The *Punch* artists, on the whole, were much better book illustrators than cartoonists. However, it is important to note that *Punch* had a tremendous impact on the basic form of graphic humor inasmuch as it was here that the captioned cartoon was perfected. Also significant was *Vanity Fair*, which published countless color lithographs by Carlo Pellegrini (Ape), Leslie Ward (Spy), and other leading caricaturists of the 1880's. And, one must not forget the virtuosity of Max Beerbohm, still the reigning prince of the distorted portrait.

German cartoons that appeared in journals such as *Fliegende Blätter* and *Kladderadatsch* were rendered in this nation's characteristically disciplined, exquisite manner. However, the form and the content were basically duplications of *Punch*, and thereby lacked authenticity and relevance. The true shining light of German graphic comedy was Wilhelm Busch, a prolific cartoonist and master of the macabre. His most popular creation, Max and Moritz, later inspired Rudolph Dirk's famous American strip, "The Katzenjammer Kids." It was not until 1896, with the publication of *Simplicissimus,* that German satire reached its zenith. The publisher, Albert Langen, inaugurated the most significant stylistic revolution in the art of satire since Daumier. *Der Simpl*'s stable of artists included graphic geniuses who redefined the act of cartooning. Their line was imbued with art nouveau decorative curves, yet their acerbic wit was devastating and often prophetic. Attacks against capitalism, industrialization and the ruling class were harsh. However, like the young jester after whom the magazine was named (a fictional character, Simplicus Simplicissimus), who invited his victims to sit in the front row and enjoy his show, *Der Simpl* appealed to the same *Junker* and upper classes it was ridiculing. The artists also exhibited great affection for the working and peasant classes and championed the "volk" spirit. *Simplicissimus* markedly influenced the work of many twentieth century expressionist artists such as Max Beckman and Georg Grosz.

In America, the first acknowledged cartoonist was none other than Benjamin Franklin (the engraver, and patriot, Paul Revere is a close second), whose "Join or Die" cartoon brilliantly symbolized the struggle of the thirteen colonies and served as a rallying point for the revolutionaries. The drawings and prints by others—mostly anonymous artists—that preceded the Civil War were often poorly-rendered, hackneyed copies of the British approach. Frank Bellew and A. Volck were among the few interesting artists of the 1850's and 60's. The foremost cartoonist of the period was Bavarian-born Thomas Nast. He changed for the better the function and form of American caricature. His influences were European and his approach was classical, yet he developed a graphic language that translated into a uniquely American style of political cartooning. His tremendous power as a commentator was rooted in his ability to motivate public opinion. Because of an unrelenting bombardment of his drawings published in *Harper's Weekly,* the corrupt New York politician Boss Tweed was forced out of office and was ultimately arrested (the drawings enabled officials to identify him).

In 1876 the chromolithic (color printing) revolution reached America from Germany and its effect upon the populace was as great as the impact that talking pictures and television had in the following century. In the vanguard of this technological explosion was the satiric weekly *Puck*, edited and chiefly illustrated by Austrian-born Joseph Keppler. Not only did *Puck* open the floodgates for scores of cartoonists of all graphic persuasions (political, burlesque and fanciful), it also spawned numerous competitors—*Judge, Verdict, Wasp* and *Chic.* This era was so alive with innovations in graphic humor that Frank Luther Mott, America's foremost magazine historian, has dubbed it "The Age of Fun."

The cartoons from this period were usually overly rendered in the classical tradition. They included details and backgrounds that betrayed a lack of ability, as well as an obvious desire to reproduce photography. Even though the artwork was laden with clichés and biblical and literary references, the cartoons had a vitriol (libelous by current standards) that frightened the politicos and excited the masses.

*Life* was another influential periodical born in *Puck*'s wake. It considered itself a sophisticated, high-brow, magazine—above the scandalous behavior of its tawdry competitors. It not only lampooned the idiosyncrasies of high and low society, but also created fads and fashions of its own. *Life*'s leading cartoonist, Charles Dana Gibson, developed the Gibson Girl (so widespread was her image that one must compare her impact on the mores of the Gilded Age to that exerted by the Beatles on the fashion and music of the sixties). *Life* prospered thanks to developments in mechanical reproduction which allowed for the halftone printing of photographs. The impact of this new technology was apparent in the loose pencil and wash drawings, many with simple backgrounds, which became a stylish manner of cartooning. The magazine employed exciting, innovative cartoonists who enjoyed popular followings (and thereby sold many copies of their cartoon anthologies): E.W. Kemble, Eugene Zimmerman, T.S. Sullivant, Harrison Cady, and Richard F. Outcault were among the most successful graphic comedians, and Fred Opper, W.A. Rogers and Art Young were sought-after political commentators. (Of note: the comic animal phenomenon, so popular today, originated with *Puck's* "Buggville" and *Life's* "Funny Animals" compendiums.) Well-known illustrators such as James Montgomery Flagg, Tony Sarge and the Leyendecker brothers tried their hands at cartooning in *Life.* As the magazine entered the Twenties, a new crop of cartoon stylists—including John Held Jr., Gluyas Williams and Rea Irvin—joined the "Staff of Life." They brought with them a deco approach to cartooning which typified the flapper years. *Life* degenerated in its final years to a collection of purile college humor gags (a form that was enjoying popularity at the time). It folded in 1929 and sold its name to Henry Luce, who later established his own milestone in the history of publishing.

By World War I, *Puck* had succumbed to the burgeoning success of the mass circulation newspaper, specifically the Sunday color supplements. The two major publishing rivals, William Randolf Hearst and Joseph Pulitzer, had managed to steal most of the good comic talent in order to produce comic-strips—the revolutionary new form of American graphic humor. Newspapers were featuring scores of editorial cartoonists on a daily basis (they were invaluable in the quest for larger circulations). Although a few of their number—Davenport, McCutcheon, Opper, Berryman and Fitzpatrick—succeeded in evoking controversial points of view with their amusing reflections on the political scene, many of the drawings produced for this medium were more editorial propaganda, dictated by the publisher, than individual satiric statements. Even Winsor McKay, the most significant (and prolific) comic strip artist, created cliché-ridden pap which ran alongside Arthur Brisbane's editorials in the Hearst papers. During this time the most insightful graphic satires were coming from the artists of *The Masses,* a socialist magazine edited by Max Eastman, devoted to art and politics. A myriad of contributors including "ash-can school" painters George Bellows, John Sloan, Stuart Davis, Adolf Dehn, Maurice Becker and Boardman Robinson created cartoons in the tradition of Daumier. Cartoonists Art Young (who was arrested three times for "seditious" cartooning), R.K. Chamberlain and Robert Minor (whose "The Perfect Soldier" is a masterpiece of protest art) were also regular staffers.

Of major significance to the history of graphic humor was the publication of *The New Yorker* in 1923 by Harold Ross. Tired of the pendantic "he/she" gags found in the college humor magazines, he created a novel graphic form, alternately called the humor cartoon, caption cartoon, and most commonly, the gag cartoon. Preferring mild social satire to political comment (although early issues had some of this as well, specifically a piece by Reginald Marsh on lynching in the South), *The New Yorker* emerged as the satiric watch-dog of high society, boy scouts, and bridge clubs, as well as being an erstwhile reporter of the human comedy. Entertainment was the fundamental intent of the magazine. Irony and economical rendering were the hallmarks of the drawings and governed the approaches of Peter Arno, Gardner Rea, Otto Soglow, James Thurber, Mary Petty and Gluyas Williams, among others. As art historian Thomas Craven points out in *Cartoon Cavalcade:* "The artists were allowed to kick up their heels joyfully, each in his own style, there being but one reservation. The editor called the tune. Individuality was exploited for all it was worth, but no artist, however gifted, could belong to the coterie unless his work conformed to the editorial pattern. The ideas and the subjects were submitted or proscribed and when the drawing was done it was instantly recognizable as something only *The New Yorker* could conceive and produce."

*The New Yorker* offered its readers a cornucopia of graphic talents—indeed it still has a stable of very astute and funny artists. Unfortunately, though, *The New Yorker* style being the most visible in America is accepted by many as the preeminent form of visual humor. As we will see it is only one approach in a larger, more diverse field.

\*　　　\*　　　\*

Graphic satire is a complex discipline not easily dismissed as fad or trend. Its practitioners over the eons have conformed to and rebelled against the artistic conventions of specific periods, often reflecting changes in the cultural fabric. We know that early caricature was practiced as a means of shocking the established order (Rembrandt created caricatures as a respite from the rigors of painting in the Grand Manner). Humorous art of the nineteenth century was wed to classical modes of draftsmanship and definitions of beauty. Virtually all the cartoonists of this period were schooled in the same practices—a reason why drawings of the era are so similar in appearance and are now dated. The first "modern" cartoonist, Rodolphe Töppfler (the father of the comic narrative sequence) worked during the 1830's and 40's. He believed that a cartoonist need not imitate nature in order to better his art. It is enough, he stated, to interpret what one sees—and feels.

As technology advanced, artists were afforded more varied means of reproducing their drawings, thus markedly effecting style. The woodcut was surpassed by the copperplate engraving, the engraving by the lithograph, the lithograph by photographic and mechanical means. By the late nineteenth century, artistic and industrial revolutions in France and Germany had already changed the look of the cartoon. Art nouveau, Arts and Crafts, Jugenstil and Symbolist approaches were evident in the drawings of Caran d'Ache, Bruno Paul, Aubrey Beardsley, and Alexander Steinlen. Modernism had an impact on a number of cultural forms—music, architecture, literature and certainly graphic humor. Cubist stylings were evident in the satiric work of Georg Grosz, Raoul Dufy and Jean Cocteau. Expressionist and cartoon approaches characterized an entire group of German artists who practiced social commentary in their prints and painterly works. Picasso was a cartoonist, appearing with other artists, later to become giants, such as Juan Gris, Felix Valloton, Keis Van Dongen, Paul Iribe, Jacques Forian and Jacques Villon in *fin de siècle* satiric periodicals *including Les Quatre Gats,* and *L'Assiette Au Beurre*. In the twenties the various Dada groups, most prominently the Berlin Dada, were definitely satiric in their approach to art and society. Otto Dix and John Heartfield created unique and powerful commentaries attacking war and facism. It is not surprising therefore, that the past two decades of graphic satire has been markedly influenced by the art of the twentieth century.

Apart from these artistic and social factors that affect and influence comic artists, there also exists an intangible force that ignites their satiric passions. Fritz Eichenberg, long a practitioner of the art, calls this power a "satiric flame," and E. H. Gombrich and Ernst Kris, in their essay on caricature in *Art and Illusion,* refer to it simply as "magic." Although this impulse is difficult to define in formalistic terms—and the artists themselves find it difficult to define with the same ease with which they can discuss a particular point of view—it is not merely a romantic notion. It is a glue that binds the cartoonist's sensitivity, individuality, and craft to the extremely personal act of satire.

The flame burns brightly in the twenty-two cartoonists who are represented in this volume. They display a wide range of painterly and graphic skills and a love of drawing. Most important, they have expanded the definition of cartooning—as Steinberg has done with his unique amalgam of abstract forms, color, and personal symbology. It is obvious that these artists pay homage to the legacy of satire—Steadman's expressionism and Levine's mannered approach are living monuments. But most significant is the debt owed to the artists here by the scores of neophytes who have "borrowed" styles, most notably from Searle, Osborn, Levine, Feiffer, Sorel and Blechman.

*Man Bites Man* is dedicated to the past masters of this craft, but more to the point, it is an appreciation of the contemporary practitioners—artists whose humor and intelligence have added so much to our understanding of the world. Displayed here are small samplings from larger collections of published and unpublished work, arranged in portfolio format. I have selected drawings produced within the past twenty years primarily because the strengths of these cartoonists shone through, elucidated and reflected the events and sensibilities of the past two explosive decades. Some of the drawings will be familiar to the aficionado of graphic satire: Levine's "Godfather Nixon" and Feiffer's "Stonewall" are reminders of the Watergate zoo. Some of the drawings have been excerpted from previously published monographs, while others will be a surprise: such as those by Sempé, Flora, and Desclozeaux which are rarely presented to American audiences. André François's work is, for the most part, a departure from what viewers here are used to. All the drawings presented are derived from markedly different sensibilities. Many of them are timeless: Searle's "The Arrival of God" and Koren's "Is It Funny?" have universal appeal. Even many of the decidedly topical cartoons transcend the moment.

This book is a celebration of satiric art from around the world. Unfortunately, sophisticated graphic humor is not as popular in the United States as it is in Europe. The satiric and comic journals which once offered so much have long since folded. *Monocle* died in 1963 (it was edited by Victor Navasky and included such graphic contributors as Sorel, Levine, Blechman, Paul Davis, Seymour Chwast, Randy Enos and Marshal Arisman). The *East Village other*, which reached its peak during the late Sixties, was virtually the last American periodical to prominently feature acerbic visual wit in the tradition of *Puck*. Regretfully The *National Lampoon* has regressed in recent years. Europe, on the other hand, especially France, Italy, Germany and England, still offers a haven for satirists. Publishers such as Albin Michel, in Paris, produce important cartoon anthologies (including work by TIM and Picha). Diogenes Verlag in Zurich has an impressive list of titles by Ungerer, Flora, Gorey and Sendak. Organizations devoted to the study of cartooning exist in France, Belgium, Canada, Bulgaria and Switzerland. The Swann Foundation for Caricature and Cartoon based in New York City is extremely viable here. Recently the Kestner-Gesellschaft and the Wilhelm Busch Museum in Hanover, West Germany presented exhibitions of drawings by contemporary satirists which met with critical acclaim. Rarely is an exhibition of this kind greeted with similar seriousness by the art establishment here. Satiric art remains a viable tool of protest, as evidenced by Amnesty International's cartoon collection entitled *Shut Up*, a selection of images attacking violations of human rights by artists from all over the globe. Satiric art in the United States is often a catch-as-catch-can proposition: Feiffer and Levine have tenure in the *Village Voice* and the *New York Review of Books*, respectively. But only the editorial cartoonists have a guaranteed space on a daily basis. Most others are bereft of any regular outlets. Periodical editors and publishers must be convinced of the viability of this form before it becomes a thing of the past seen only in nostalgic exhibitions.

*    *    *

I have chosen the artists in this book because I am an admirer—more accurately I am a fan—of their work, and, have been inspired by their humor. I have followed Feiffer's strips both in the *Voice* and through syndication—often they articulate my own unspoken frustrations with the *system*. I will always find a different week's statement posted on someone's wall or on a merchant's cash register attesting to Feiffer's appeal. I was weaned on the caricatures of Levine and Ed Sorel—their acerbic critical "portraits" of sacrosanct politicians and religionists exposed the blemishes of all those people who were seemingly above reproach. The comic travelogues—regular fare in the pages of *Holiday*—afforded my first glimpse at the brilliance of Ronald Searle. Gahan Wilson's macabre fantasies have always been the high point of *Playboy's* cartoon selection. I was addicted to all Harvey Kurtzman-edited publications—*Mad, Trump, Help* and *Humbug* where I found the lunacy of Arnold Roth. The first time I ever saw a Blechman cartoon was in *Humbug*, as well: it was a wonderful sequence entitled "White Christmas," in which a black family moves into into a white neighborhood and are greeted by a burning cross. It begins to snow, the snow smothers the flames and covers the cross with a white mound which the family proceeds to carve into a snowman—to the shock of their racist neighbors. Such a statement was virtually unheard of in lily-white 1958. The events of the sixties fostered a minor renaissance of political illustration from which Tomi Ungerer and Ralph Steadman emerged to attack the senses with a panoply of graphic comments that screamed out truths about the Vietnam war and other social diseases. Also during this time, when the New Yorker graphic virtuosity was waning, Edward Koren and George Booth appeared and reshaped the image of the cartoon. A multitude of Edward Gorey stories—sardonic little books drawn in Victorian splendor—filled my bookshelves at this time. Lou Myers caught my eye and dragged me into the pages of *Monocle* with his savagely funny cartoons. André François's delightful *New Yorker* covers adorned my wall as did the drawing on page 64, which I was pleased to obtain for this book. As an art director I have worked closely with Hans Georg Rauch, Eugene Mihaesco, Bill Lee and Pierre Le-Tan—their work is exemplary of the diversity in comic art. I have admired Sempé, Declozeaux and Flora from afar and am very happy to have them in this volume. Most recently I was reintroduced to the remarkable work of Robert Osborn. His albums display an uncompromised commitment to moral conscience, brilliantly conveyed.

Thanks to these artists my passion for the art of graphic satire has not ebbed. It is my hope you will also come away shouting their praises.

Blechman

BOOTH.

desclozeaux

Jules Feiffer

André François

FLORA

Edward Gorey

Koren

Bill lee

Pierre Le-Tan

D. Levine

# Blechman

If one believes what the late cartoonist J. N. Darling said about the cartoon, that "it is a humor-coated capsule by means of which the sober judgments of editorial minds may be surreptitiously gotten down the throats of an apathetic public," then R. O. Blechman's drawings are, indeed, very potent pills. He is a cartoonist whose style is without precedent: he is the master of the nervous squiggle. His deceivingly simple graphic approach is wily camouflouge for the many social and political satires that comprise his oeuvre.

Since his satiric impulse was operative much earlier in his career, it is ironic that Blechman is best known today for his commercial work. At a young age he discovered that he had a need to dissent, a need best articulated through cartooning. His draftsmanship was poor at the time, and were it not for a quick wit and the ability to conceive ideas effortlessly, his work might never have seen the light of day. No matter how deficient his graphic prowess appeared, Blechman believed that the desire to speak out on the issues of the day would eventually find the proper graphic vehicle. In 1949 while still in college, he began to publish drawings. He recalls that he was afraid of his facility for making outrageous statements, and the apprehension that developed was, in part, responsible for his decision to draw in miniature. Meanwhile, two conflicting personality traits appeared in his work—that of the self-effacing introvert and that of the boisterous extrovert. The latter accounts for the delicate line which serves as a counterpoint to his ironic commentaries. Of this dichotomy he simply states: "Watch out for the sweet person—there is a lot of anger behind the facade."

Blechman rarely creates partisan political commentary. He prefers instead to be an outsider, if for no other reason than to support the underdog. A compulsion to do things out of the mainstream explains his radical departure from the stiff, mannered illustration style of the fifties and early sixties.

Although he insists that reason and art do not make the happiest bedfellows, he is extremely rational in his view of cartooning: "I can never portray a black villain or a white hero; they are only gray. One slides into villainy as the other slides into heroism"—an interesting notion in relation to cartooning, illustrated here in his strip "The Death of Judas."

In the manner of the court jester, Blechman attacks social absurdity with comic absurdity. His art is a weapon that disarms the viewer through humor and then invades the senses. Blechman believes that acts of social satire and political commentary are occasions for making larger statements about people who are trapped by forces beyond their control. He understands the potency of protest art: "When one sees Goya's *Disasters of War,* the response is not rage against Napoleon but a disgust at what humans will do to other humans." However, he is skeptical with regard to the ultimate influence subtle satire has on political realities: "When Chaplin makes a social comment through humor, people for the most part just see the humor. On the other hand, when Upton Sinclair wrote with graphic detail about the stockyards and slaughterhouses in Chicago, the result was the Pure Food and Drug Laws."

Blechman is by no means a burlesque comic. He is not interested in making people laugh at entertaining diversions—that response can be achieved through simpler forms of humor. His focus is on creating fresh, provocative statements ("I'd rather make George Booth laugh"), and so he is always pushing the limits of his medium. The characters in his early work were amorphous—male things and female things, ageless and shapeless. Now they are more complex, able to express a wide range of emotions. Often it takes hours to draw the most expressive squiggle. His compositions are meticulously planned, for Blechman feels that a line out of place or a horizon too high can cause the cartoon to fail. He is a perfectionist in a medium that is basically a sketcher's paradise.

**HEADING FOR THE LAST HIBERNATION**
*R. O. Blechman/1975*

**A HISTORY OF HALLOWEEN**

*R. O. Blechman/1976*

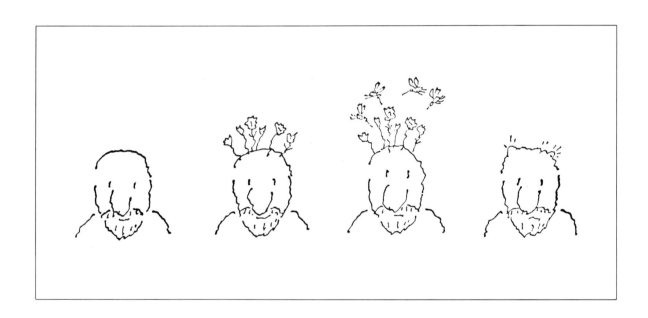

**FREUD'S DISASTER WITH COCAINE**

*R. O. Blechman/1972*

OVER 17 BILLION SERVED

*R. O. Blechman/1974*

**THE DROP OUT GENERATION**

*R. O. Blechman/1973*

**THE DEATH OF JUDAS**

*R. O. Blechman/1978*

# BOOTH.

Few single-panel cartoonists have accomplished what the strip artists do as a matter of course: create comic characters with lives of their own. George Booth does, and thus joins Otto Soglow, Charles Addams, and George Price as a member of an exclusive club. Booth is the producer, director, and friend of a ripsnorting troup of eccentrics (both old and young): auto mechanics, hash-parlor restauranteurs, preachers, kings and queens, bull terriers, et al. He stages, choreographs, and designs his own productions—usually presented on the pages of *The New Yorker*—applying careful attention to the details of scenery and backgrounds that derive from his depression childhood. They include diners, garages, living rooms, kitchens, and porches all with bare light bulbs, naked floorboards, and pots and pans in disarray.

The captions for these drawings are beautifully composed monologues, some borrowed from Shakespeare, the *New York Times,* the *Wall Street Journal,* and other literary and journalistic sources. His wife, Dione, keeps her eyes open for potential additions to the repertoire. And Booth just keeps on creating—sometimes ten delightful panels a week.

Booth was raised in Fairfax, Missouri. He acquired both a love of drawing and a passion for people from his parents. On her vacations his mother would do cartoons for the local morning paper. (Today, under the name MawMaw Booth, she has a weekly drawing in the *Princeton Post-Telegraph.)* When he was nine years old, his first piece was published in a St. Joseph newspaper. He was inspired by the "Alley Oop" and "Cherokee Turkey" comic strips. In 1946 he began to do cartoons for the Marine Corps magazine *Leatherneck,* where he developed Spot, whom he describes as "a dog who thought he was people. People thought he was a sex-mad mongrel because he whistled at girls and rode with them in convertibles." In 1958, unable to sell enough cartoons to make a living, he accepted a position as art director for a publisher of business magazines. When he left that position after nine years, he decided to make a stab at *The New Yorker* (he had tried and failed many years before). They saw his potential, bought his drawings, and placed him under contract. His work has appeared there regularly since 1970.

For Booth the act of cartooning requires the discipline and structure he enjoys. But his foremost love is the creation of characters and situations: "Mrs. Ritterhouse is based on the strengths of my mother." He favors the pit bull and the cats, and a very special character is his "poor soul"—the fellow with the big nose and little moustache who pops up in many cartoons. Old Jesse is the mechanic "whose mind is closed like a steel trap. He's the one who knows what's wrong with the car and won't tell unless someone asks him."

Because he was a maverick in the cartoon world, Booth's drawings were always difficult to sell. However, he decided long ago just to do 100 percent Booth, and whoever wanted it could have it. "I drew for my parents' generation because I had been so entertained by their humor. Their generation laughed at life whether it was the Depression or the 1980's. I didn't see folks my age or younger laughing at life. It was a pleasant surprise when I found that my audience spanned the generations."

Booth believes that his responsibility as a cartoonist is to give people a regular laugh if he can. And he does so with aplomb. His meticulous renderings are accomplished with a Bic pen—from which he achieves "controlled accidents." He will, however, paste and repaste faces on dogs, cats, and people if the originals aren't right. He is a master of his medium and works expressly for the camera. Each printed panel is a remarkably fresh idea. He is always experimenting with subject matter and with scale. "The only thing I like better than a Booth cartoon," he says, "is a Booth cartoon big." And so he has submitted some novel multipaged sequences to *The New Yorker*—such as "IP," a study in caveman language and logic which elicited hundreds of letters of praise from the readers of the magazine. "As I.F. Stone said, I feel so happy doing what I do that I should be arrested." When people ask me what I do, I say I'm a cartoonist. They say, 'Don't call yourself that, you're a caricaturist.' I'm not a caracaturist. Whether cartooning as I do it is art or not, I don't care; it's what I do and I enjoy it."

"Having concluded, your Highness, an exhaustive study of this nation's political, social, and economic history, and after examining, Sire, the unfortunate events leading to the present deplorable state of the realm, the consensus of the Council is that your Majesty's only course, for the public good, must be to take the next step."

*George Booth/1975*

*George Booth/1974*

*"I call this spot Templeton's end, because this is where I dumped Old Templeton in the bog—Newport wheelchair and all."*

"I've got an idea for a story: Gus and Ethel live on Long Island, on the North Shore. He works sixteen hours a day writing fiction. Ethel never goes out, never does anything except fix Gus sandwiches, and in the end she becomes a nympho-lesbo-killer-whore. Here's your sandwich."

"Three years in a row, Hoot's lespedeza went moldy. His chickens got sick and quit laying. He tried mixing his own anti-freeze and busted both tractor blocks. Then Coolidge, his favorite mule, slipped in the barn lot and died. It just seemed like one bad omen after another. So finally Hoot says, 'It's either shoot the cattle or run for Congress.' Well, Hoot ain't one to shoot animals, but you can bet your bottom dollar he'll tell those other congressmen what's up there in Washington."

*George Booth/1974*

*"One of you boys go help Mom with the groceries."*

*George Booth/1978*

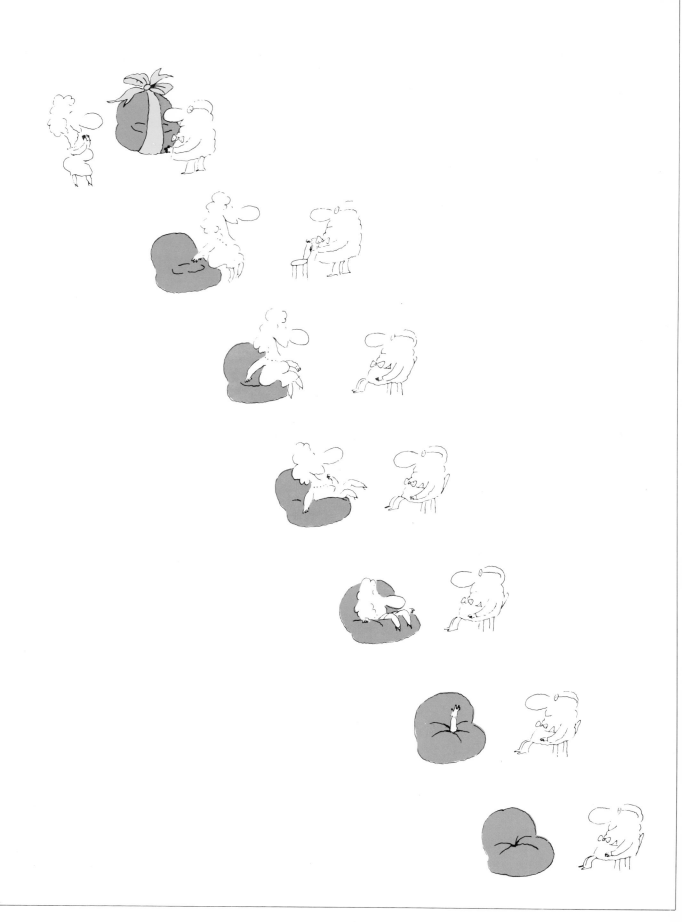

*Jean-Pierre Desclozeaux/1973*

# desclozeaux

A good cartoonist is a magician who excites his audience with a myriad of surprising images and ideas. Jean-Pierre Desclozeaux is an exemplary illusionist whose very being is something unexpected. His Lilliputian cartoons are in marked contrast to their creator—a large, stolid, bearded man whose devotion to the miniature is pervasive in all aspects of his life. He resides in a small apartment, works in a tiny studio, and derives pleasure from a collection of precision-made, antiquarian toys. Like the artist, the work is rife with contextual contradictions (while remaining stylistically consistent): On the one hand, delightful sentimentality abounds; on the other, his lucid commentaries have a venomous side, albeit one that is cloaked and guarded. The former is manifest in the playful, decidedly optimistic drawings—pastel hearts, colorful feathered quills, bright suns, and fanciful animals—featured on numerous greeting cards with his imprimatur. The latter are often critical side glances describing social conditions—relations between man and woman, people and environment, war and peace—by means of allusion.

Desclozeaux has an agile mind that is successfully visualized through his graphic shorthand. Although he appears to be a doodler, his drawings are made with a highly disciplined application of linear and color expertise. He can articulate an expression or describe an emotion with a minimum of effort—he draws the sense without drawing the whole thing. He has a wealth of symbols at his fingertips which are particularly French, yet speak of universal issues. Often his more trenchant statements begin in graphic exercises that bring forth disparate objects in a freely associative manner (such as the alligator and dove and the airplane and cityscape metaphors which appear in this portfolio). Turning the pages on the world of Desclozeaux is like romping through a funhouse, never knowing what titillating astonishment is around the next corner.

Desclozeaux was born in Sernhac (in the Gard), France, and went to school in Avignon. He began a three-year apprenticeship in Paris with the famed poster artist Paul Colin in 1957. His career as a professional cartoonist commenced shortly thereafter. He was the founder of the Society for the Protection of Humor (which has sponsored exhibitions and books) and has remained its president for many years. He created theater posters and an animated weekly cartoon for the *Nouvel Observateur* that continues today.

His work derives from a tradition of modern French cartoonists, epitomized by Chaval (Yvan Le Louarn) and Jean Maurice Bosc, that ignores individual characterizations and focuses on staging comic situations. Unlike his freer cartoons—which are not strictly speaking cartoons at all, but rather nonverbal, self-contained vignettes—his topical drawings are incisive illustrations that emphasize, and at times analyze, substantive world and regional events. His illustration assignments often result in a productive alliance of restraint and imagination. For instance, a booklet he designed for French cardiologists entitled "Life Style of a Heart Attack Victim" offered Desclozeaux a wonderful challenge to be both comic and insightful with a difficult subject, and to enliven a serious matter without being inaccessible. A favorite vehicle of expression is the miniature book (short on pages, large on energy). Often these gems are privately printed to honor a special occasion and mailed to friends as Christmas or birthday cards, or just for the fun of it. They are exquisitely produced, sardonic pantomimes enhanced by a filmmaker's pacing and a storyteller's timing. A particularly rare example, which is deceptively innocent, is accompanied by a brief text: "There once was a little lamb;/Too much a dreamer; too pacifist; too polite; too timid; too naive; too credulous; too playful;/In brief he was too tender to avoid being eaten." At such times the dark side of Desclozeaux sneaks up from behind and leaves its mark.

Jean-Pierre Desclozeaux/1972

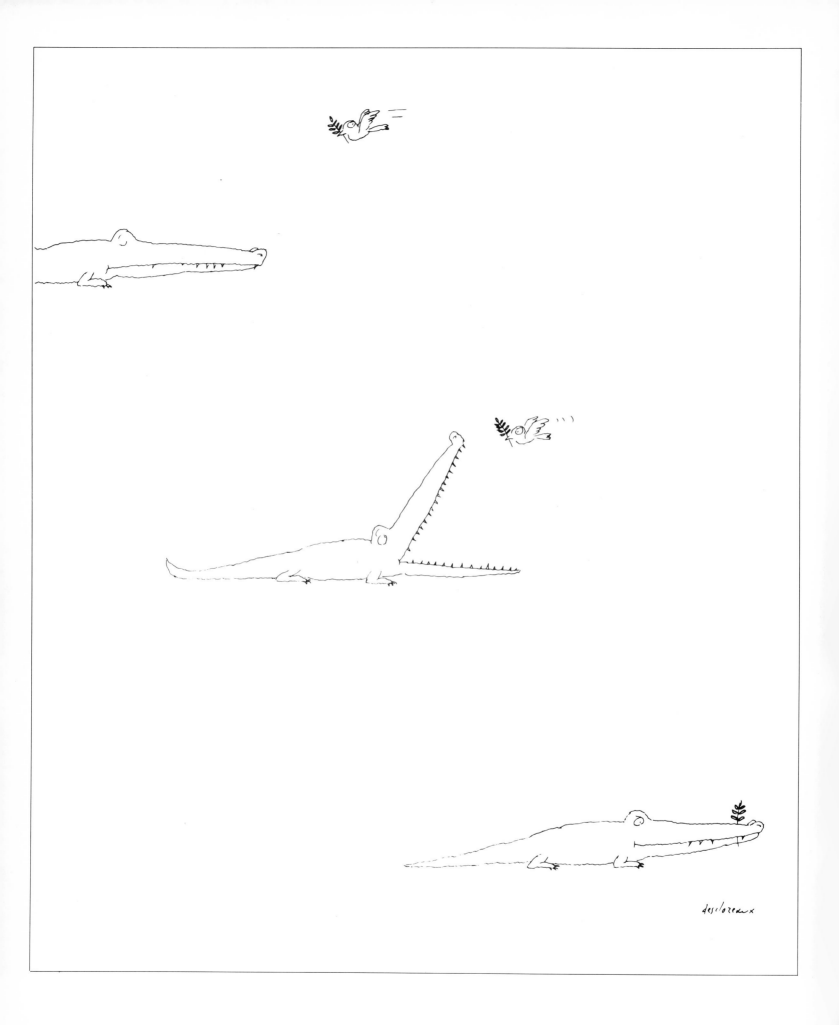

Jean-Pierre Desclozeaux/1972

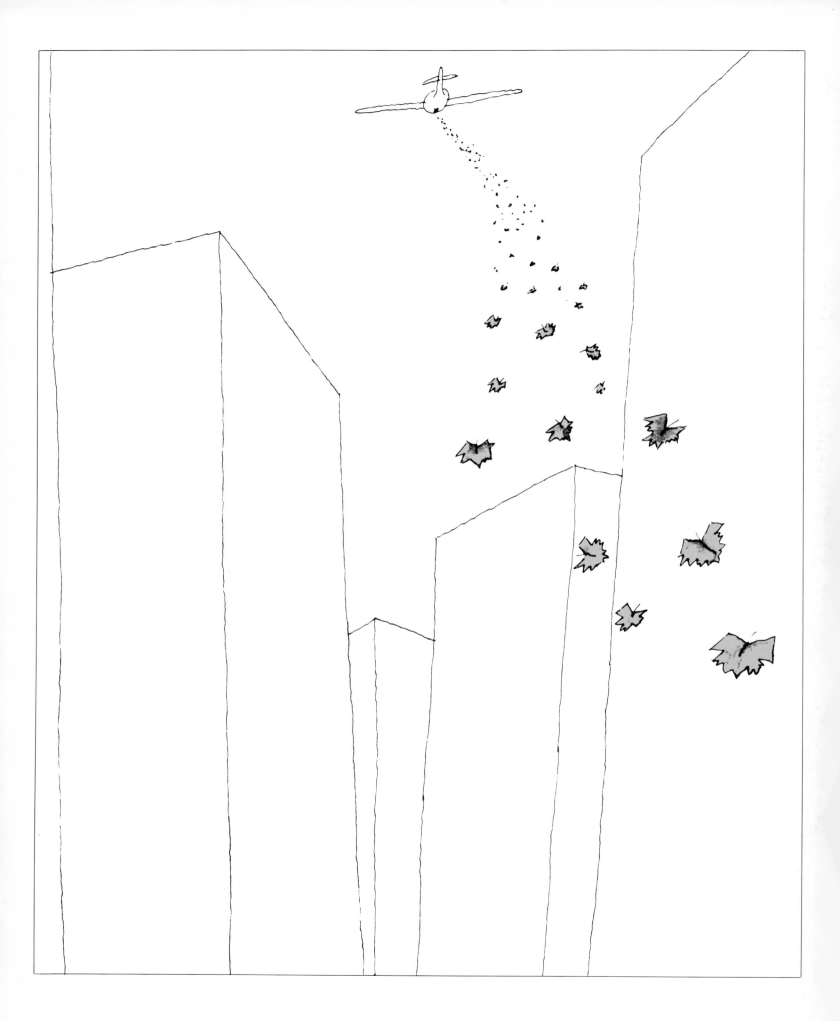

**L'AVION DE L'AUTOME**

*Jean-Pierre Desclozeaux/1966*

*Jean-Pierre Desclozeaux/1980*

Jean-Pierre Desclozeaux/1967

WHEN THEY DRAGGED ME TO SCHOOL AT 5, I REMEMBER SCREAMING: **BUT I'M NOT READY**

WHEN THEY SENT ME TO CAMP AT 10, I REMEMBER SCREAMING: **BUT I'M NOT READY!**

©1974 JULES FEIFFER 9-22

WHEN THEY DRAFTED ME AT 19, I REMEMBER SCREAMING: **BUT I'M NOT READY!**

WHEN THEY MARRIED ME OFF AT 23, I REMEMBER SCREAMING: **BUT I'M NOT READY!**

WHEN THEY MADE ME A FATHER AT 24, 25, 26 AND 27 I REMEMBER SCREAMING: **BUT I'M NOT READY — NOT READY NOT READY NOT READY!**

FINALLY, AT 50, I RAN AWAY FROM MY WIFE, MY KIDS AND MY GRANDCHILDREN.

I'M NOT COMING OUT AGAIN TILL I'M READY.

DADDY! GRANPA! GEORGE!

*Jules Feiffer/1974*

_Jules Feiffer_ [signature]

Jules Feiffer came on the scene as the bubble of repression nurtured during the fifties was ready to burst. Suffering through Joseph McCarthy and the pervasive conformity of the Eisenhower years, the post-World War II generation was hungry for a spokesman. Humor was the great equalizer, and Feiffer was a formidable practitioner. Like his contemporaries Mort Sahl, Lenny Bruce, and Mike Nichols and Elaine May, he opened a Pandora's box of social, political, and psychological issues and addressed them graphically in the critical tradition of the Weimar cabaret. Feiffer, further, redefined the form of the comic strip by readjusting the "camera eye," demolishing panel walls and speech balloons. He markedly influenced the content of the editorial cartoon by injecting a decidedly personal attitude in place of clichéd symbolism. He combined an innocent drawing style with a scenarist's mastery of language, thereby affording himself a tool with which to synthesize complex situations into six or eight insightful sequences. Of this sensitivity, Victor Navasky says, "Feiffer's remarkable inner ear gives him that marvelous ability...to speak with the language of ordinary people in an extraordinary way."

Feiffer spent his childhood in the East Bronx, New York. He grew up in a world of socialist politics and comic strips. Except for art classes, his idea of school was to mark time until he got into the comic-strip business. His "idols" included Winsor McCay, Will Eisner, and Milton Caniff. Instead of going to college, he applied for work with Will Eisner: "He told me that I showed no talent at all, but all the same he gave me a job erasing and filling in blacks. I was so excited I hyperventilated all the way home." Drafted in 1951, his rebellion surfaced: "I was ripped away from my family for the first time. I was treated with open contempt by one form of authority or another." He wrote three cartoon books: _Munro,_ about a four-year-old boy drafted into the army by mistake; _Boom,_ a satire on the bomb; and _Sick, Sick, Sick,_ which in 1956 was the first set of strips regularly published in the _Village Voice_ (acting as a philanthropist, he gave it to them for free). It was subsequently picked up by the _London Observer_ and then put into syndication. He also began working for _Playboy._ Among Feiffer's literary influences stand Beckett and Robert Benchley: "What I had wanted to do was take the humor that Benchley was famous for and show how his little man functioned in the fifties." He subsequently developed Bernard Mergendeiler, a semiautobiographical character who lives in and reflects upon a modern Freudian world.

Throughout the sixties Feiffer was particularly attuned to politics. Walt Kelly was a great influence; rage was an important motivator. In 1963 he was the first cartoonist to come out against the Vietnam War. His strip was moved from the editorial to the comic pages of the _New York Post_ because of his strong position. He covered the Chicago conspiracy trial with savage accuracy and he continues to pinpoint the folly of his political foes with unequaled insight—the combination of words and caricature in his hands is a powerful weapon.

When one considers his weekly cartoons, novels, plays, and screenplays, Feiffer stands as the most prolific social commentator of the past two decades. His work reflects myriad concerns. In 1967 he wrote the play _Little Murders,_ the story of a New York family's struggle with the horrors and absurdity of city life. Feiffer's _White House Murder Case_ is a provocative play concerning a United States war against Brazil, the use of nerve gas there, the cover-up back home, and the murder of the President's wife. A cartoon he did in 1965 about the neutron bomb predates any public recognition of its existence. In 1971 he wrote the screenplay for _Carnal Knowledge_—the sexual odyssey of two men from youth to middle age—and, in 1975 _Knock, Knock_ was produced on Broadway. Recently he did the screenplay for the film _Popeye,_ in which his love of the Segar strip and his passion for complex characterization are evidenced.

Feiffer has truly been a significant and accurate spokesman for two generations of artists and viewers. It is no wonder that many people have uttered the phrase: "I felt like a character in a Feiffer cartoon."

I STONEWALLED THEM ON THE WAR.

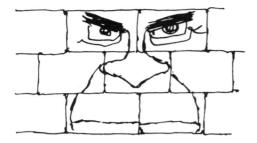

I STONEWALLED THEM ON THE COVER-UP.

I STONEWALLED THEM ON THE TAXES.

I STONEWALLED THEM ON THE TAPES.

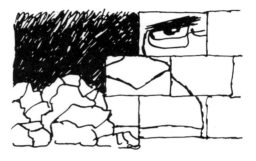

I STONEWALLED THEM ON THE COURTS.

I HAVE NOT YET BEGUN TO STONEWALL.

© 1974 Jules Feiffer 8-19

*Jules Feiffer/1974*

# WHO LOST VIET NAM?

"NOT I," SAID IKE. "I JUST SENT MONEY."

"NOT I," SAID JACK. "I JUST SENT ADVISORS."

"NOT I," SAID LYNDON. "I JUST FOLLOWED JACK."

"NOT I," SAID DICK. "I JUST HONORED JACK AND LYNDON'S COMMITMENTS."

"NOT I," SAID JERRY. "WHAT WAS THE QUESTION?"

"**YOU** LOST VIETNAM," SAID HENRY, "BECAUSE YOU DIDN'T TRUST YOUR LEADERS."

6-8 ©1975 Jules Feiffer

*Jules Feiffer/1975*

*Jules Feiffer/1975*

I LIVE INSIDE A SHELL

THAT IS INSIDE A WALL

THAT IS INSIDE A FORT

THAT IS INSIDE A TUNNEL

THAT IS UNDER THE SEA

WHERE I AM SAFE

FROM YOU.

IF YOU REALLY LOVED ME
YOUD FIND ME.

       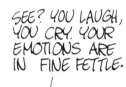 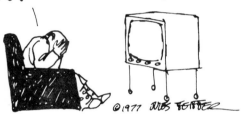

  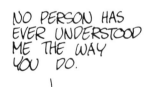  

*Jules Feiffer/1977*

Jules Feiffer/1979

Paul Flora/1974

# FLORA

Paul Flora enjoys an impressive reputation among his German, Austrian, and Swiss admirers. Since his present work is neither gag nor narrative, his humor is often inaccessible to American viewers, who are used to panel and strip cartooning. However, when he is playful, as in the albums *Flora's Fauna* and *Penthouse,* and allows his associative wit the necessary freedom to flower, the resultant comedy appeals to all. Many of his drawings are vignettes set in mythical kingdoms, grand plazas, or seedy urban settings where the absurd is commonplace. He is not a surrealist, even though the dreamlike juxtaposition of reality and fantasy is an important device in his work. His imaginative approach to satire derives from a tradition of the macabre, exemplified by the Austrian fantasist Alfred Kubin, whose bizarre *fin de siecle* work defies scholarly categorization. Similarly, it is difficult to place Flora into a comfortable mold. His drawings are imbued with a symbolist's sensitivity, but classical allegory is rejected in favor of a unique, personal vocabulary. His cartoons are rendered in two distinct manners: those with minimal, sketchy lines that evoke immediate, comic response, and those with more intricate cross-hatchings which set the stage for a larger drama. "When a drawing dominates the idea," he says, "that is a well-done drawing. Visual satire is always more successful when it speaks without overly literal supports." Flora enjoys working with pictorial exotica—images of kings, clerics, vampires, Victorian structures, skeletons, birds, domineering women—in which political undertones abound. Since he has not created overt political commentary for a few years ("This form did not offer me enough independence"), a Flora metaphor allows the viewer to affix his own interpretation. He is a humorist in an intellectual mode—a witty combination of Steinberg and Thurber. His success in transmitting acerbic, yet subtle, comic statements through his probing line is comparable to the work of Lyonel Feininger and Paul Klee—his two most important influences. But Flora's love of drawing supersedes all other explanations of his work. He speaks for many artists when he says: "While others have to pay their psychiatrists, I am lucky to make money doing my own therapy."

Flora is an Austrian citizen, born in 1922 in Glorenza, Italy. He attended school in Innsbruck and later studied at the Munich Academy under Olaf Gulbranson (onetime *Simplicissimus* contributor and the master of modern caricature). After serving in the military, he established himself as a freelance artist and was published in major periodicals throughout the German-speaking world. During the fifties he created many albums, including *The Steed of Muses, The War Horse,* and *People and Other Animals.* In 1957 he was engaged to do regular political cartoons for the weekly *Die Zeit.* In the sixties he retreated from the rigors of political cartooning by working on albums that reflected his personal, rather than worldly, concerns. His most recent thematic collection, *Penthouse,* is an eerie view from above: a look down on the rooftops of modern office buildings at hidden worlds of Flora's making. These contemporary towers of Babel are topped by small cities including adobe huts, Victorian cemeteries, Catholic monasteries, treehouses inhabited by hermits, and summer cottages with gardeners at work. Flora's allergory sets clear limits for our technological age. No matter how high society climbs, grace is never easy to attain.

Flora has developed considerably since his early cartoons, which were primarily sight gags, rendered in the economical European manner. His drawings now exhibit a respect for the complexities of language. In fact, many of his cartoons—in which letter forms are strapped to the backs of soldiers and entire alphabets march in single file aboard a ship of doom—are attacks on its rampant misuse. His current preoccupation is with formal art problems—texture and composition. His ideas often come from mental exercises: "For one of my drawings I was interested in drawing a raven. While making sketches of the bird, I imagined St. Marcus' Place in Venice, where many pigeons congregate. I saw Richard Wagner standing there feeding these birds, which soon became ravens in my mind's eye. This associative process is the best way in which to describe my process of creating drawings."

**BONAPART AT THE PYRAMIDS**
*Paul Flora/1962*

**THE SURVIVOR**

*Paul Flora/1973*

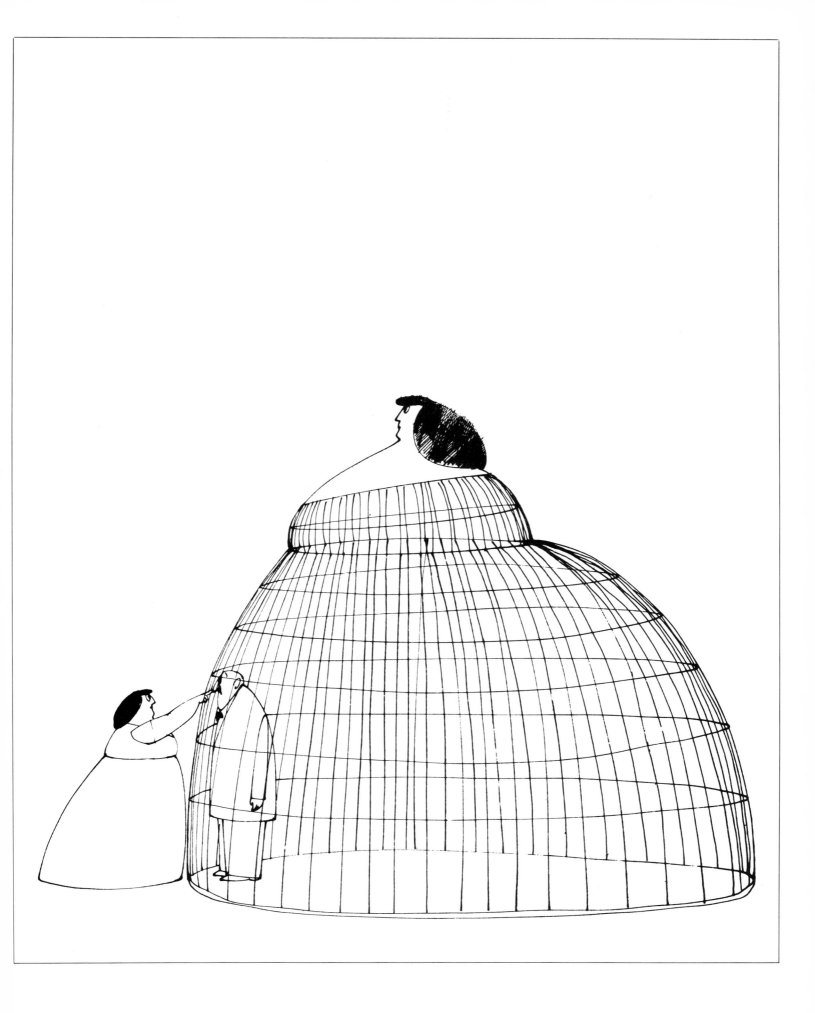

**LOVE STORY**
*Paul Flora/1972*

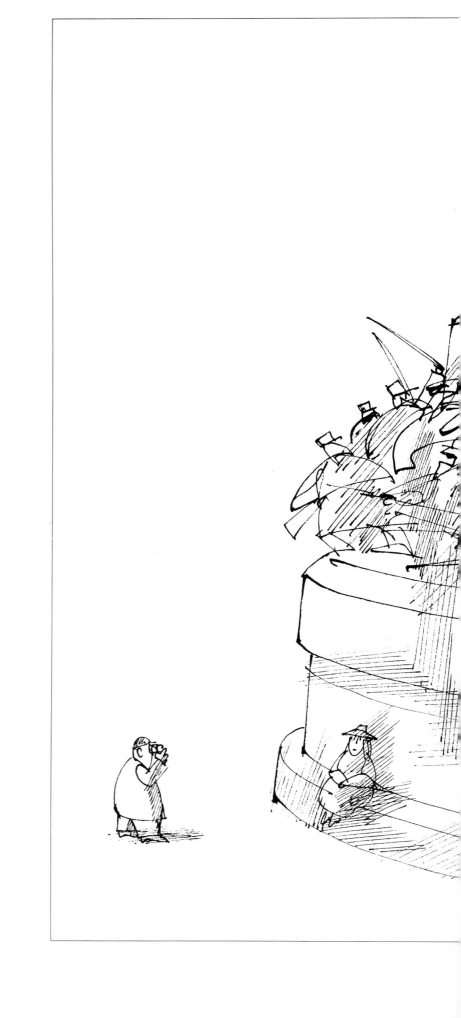

**MONUMENT FOR HEROS**

*Paul Flora/1971*

**WAGNER AND THE DISAPPEARING MOON**

*Paul Flora / 1979*

**TO HELL**

*Paul Flora/1979*

**DEPARTMENT OF THE INTERIOR**
*André François/1962*

# André François

Of André François, Walt Kelly once wrote: "He is a man beset with ideas. He seems to capture an idea with a pounce. He throws it to the ground in a frenzy, hacking at it with quick strokes to delineate its likeness. He never waits to pretty it up, smoothing its fur or arranging its limbs with the decency due unto death. His ideas are never mummified in technique or stuffed, or tanned and stretched. They are not fossils of style, and therefore François is a great man because he does as much as can be done for us stay-at-homes." Ronald Searle, another fervent admirer, has said: "It might be argued that François deliberately places himself at a disadvantage by eschewing the sensitive line in favor of the harsh scratch; that he brushes aside popular sympathy by erecting round his work a barrier of barbs. But this crude line conceals a delicate lance which can be either lethal or deflating. And herein lies his strength—whether the point goes deep or just tickles the fancy, he has the advantage of the unexpected and the mastery of surprise." And, as it is etched onto the pages of the formidable *Petit Larousse Illustré:* "He creates a world of teasing absurdity in which the dimension of the dream is integrated in things of everyday." In short, François is a forceful artist—the quintessence of graphic deception—whose universe, childlike in appearance, is a highly developed, straightforward world of visual comedies and satires on themes as varied in number as his art is elastic in form.

François was born in Rumania, a country in which the absurd is a religion—a spiritual presence found in the genes, the blood, and the mind. He left his birthplace to study at the Beaux Arts in Paris, and, fortunately for us all, the aforementioned obsessions were not left behind at Customs. He subsequently established residence in Paris, where he focused on black-and-white drawing and experimented in various areas of graphic design. Painting too soon became both a love and a profession. He was celebrated for all manner of commercial work in which he maintained the same wit and sensitivity as in his personal expressions. François's prolific creations, which adorned countless magazine pages and covers throughout the fifties and sixties, influenced and dominated the visual stylings of scores of enthusiasts (including some artists in this volume). And why not? The graphic freshness and verve he achieved through a happy abandon and the aid of the scratchiest pen nibs available afforded a higher, yet earthly, plane on which to create illustration and satire—and offered an alternative to the cliché-riddled surrealist vocabulary.

Black is not the only range on the humor spectrum practiced by François. He can be as diabolical as he can be serene. He can be playful (as evidenced by his anthropomorphics in this portfolio) or devastating. He is a comic of great range: satirist, reporter, artisan, and craftsman—free from the strictures of any one all-inclusive label. He creates commentary on the passing social scene (the drawing on page 69 is as true a record of life in New York City today as when it was composed many years ago), and on what passes for culture. He reflects upon his innermost fantasies—and it is his fanciful imagination that makes the drawings and paintings so compelling. Searle once described François's unconventional logic this way: "Driving one night with François through the darkness of a country road, the beam of his headlamps picked out two lovers walking arm in arm. As we approached them he flicked off his lights. 'Did you see?' he said, 'I made them disappear.' For a moment his dip-switch was a magical thing that metamorphosed images on the road....as with his dip-switch, so with his pen."

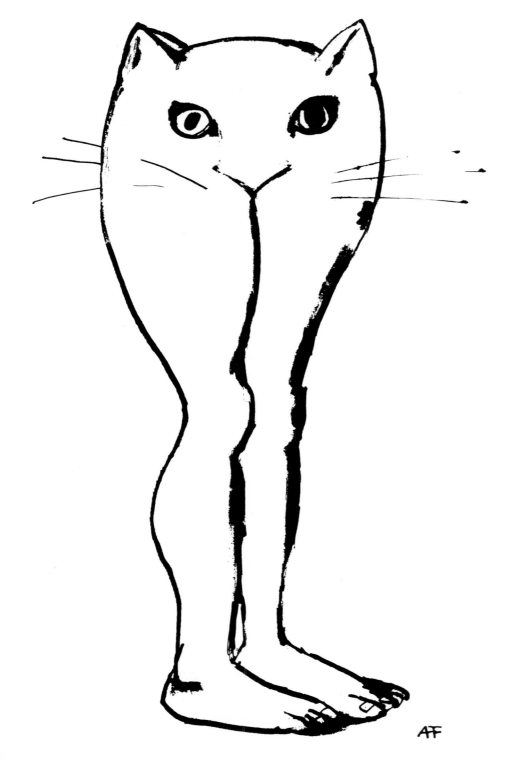

*André François/1966*

*André François/1974*

*Andrè François/1966*

*André François/1965*

*André François/1969*

*André François/1974*

*Andre François/1969 (opposite page 1976)*

Little Zooks, of whom no one was fond,

They shot towards the roof and beyond;

The infant's trajectory passed him over the rectory,

And into a lily-choked pond.

**A LIMERICK**

*Edward Gorey/1973*

# Edward Gorey

In 1959 Edmund Wilson compared Edward Gorey's achievements to those of Ronald Searle and Max Ernst. He attributed Gorey's lack of popular status at the time to the fact that he was working "quite perversely to please himself." He went on to say that the world that Gorey has created is "amusing and somber, nostalgic and claustrophobic, and the same time poetic and poisoned." Gorey is the master of an engaging—albeit thoroughly bizarre—universe governed by mystery, irony, and comic intrigue. His mode of expression is that of the nineteenth-century engraver. His meticulous linear control, combined with an acute sense of the British idiom, produces a theatrical graphic setting of Victorian rooms with overstuffed couches, ubiquitous urns, and lugubrious draperies. Here staid Edwardian ladies and gentlemen and diabolically innocent children parody the manners of that obsessively moral time—and, by extension, the absurdities of the present. Gorey's humor is an amalgam of complex sensibilities. He craftily encompasses pun, parody, and satire in works that are neither overtly political (the last time Gorey was involved with politics was during the Adlai Stevenson campaign, leaving him terribly "unstrung") nor socially focused (although he has been known to create a caustic commentary or two for the *New York Times*). He just seems to indulge in passions and eccentricities that appeal to his nature. "I started doing what I was doing," he says, "before I knew what it was."

Edward St. John Gorey was born in Chicago. He exhibited youthful artistic tendencies, but did not engage in any formal training. He served time in the Army and subsequently went to Harvard, where he began to write and draw. He prefers to think of himself as a writer: "I'm very nervous until I get the story down on paper; the drawings come easily." His influences were definitely nineteenth century; however, it was, the *twentieth-century* artist Max Ernst who "made us see that way forever." It wasn't until later that he saw the macabre children's stories of Wilhelm Busch—those and Tenniel's illustrations for *Alice in Wonderland* were inspiring. He explains his desire to parody as an homage: "If I like something very much, the impulse is to imitate."

He moved to New York City in 1953 and worked in the art department of Doubleday & Company. The book covers from this period are Gorey's unmistakable typographical creations. At this time he sold his first book, *The Unstrung Harp, or Mr. Earbrass Writes a Novel*. A thirty-page novel about writing a novel. It details with tongue-in-cheek compassion the tedious life of Mr. Clavius Frederick Earbrass, a pathetic figure in a fur coat who lives alone in a stately house full of portraits and statuettes that look exactly like him. (The book begins on November 18, a starting point for many of Gorey's novels.) Since 1953 he has produced approximately fifty small volumes, all accompanied by ironic, whimsical, and ofttimes sadistic texts. At first they were bought by a small but devoted following. But now, thanks to the efforts of Andreas Brown of the Gotham Book Mart, Gorey's stories are world-renowned.

Gorey's character is wedded to his work. His apartment in New York City is clouded by the same gray that pervades his drawings. He is fascinated by true-life tales of horror. One of his recent books, *The Loathsome Couple*, is based on a real account of a suburban English couple who murdered their children and tape-recorded their agony: "It affected me like nothing else did." The fictional authors of his tales are anagrams of his own name: Ogdred Weary, Wardor Edgy, and Drew Dogyear. He enjoys wearing the accouterments of his characters: big fur coats and sneakers. "The drawings feed reality and the reality feeds the drawings."

Gorey's most apparent satiric attack on morals and manners is in *The Curious Sofa: A Pornographic Work*, in which a young woman is exposed to all manner of sexual acts that the viewer never sees or reads—it's all left to the imagination. Gorey admits to being hostile. But when asked by a friend, the writer Alexander Theroux, why his work almost invariably focuses on violence, Gorey responded: "I don't think of myself as macabre. I write about real life."

Little Henry Clump was scarcely three years old when he found out that his heart was wicked, but that God loved him nevertheless.

He soon learnt a great many texts and hymns, and was always saying them over to himself.

Once when he saw a sea-gull rise up from the waves 'Look, look!' he said to his sister, Fanny Eliza. 'When I die I shall go up to heaven like that bird.'

He habitually went without sweet things so that he might give pennies to stop the poor heathen from bowing down to idols.

He dearly loved his parents and never tired of asking what he might do for them.

Although he was kind and good, he was sometimes tempted by Satan, but he felt his sins deeply and was truly sorry for them afterwards.

He was often discovered alone upstairs on his knees.

One Sunday he saw some boys sliding on the ice; he went up to them and said 'Oh, what a shame it is for you to idle on the Sabbath instead of reading your Bibles!'

He was very fond of Fanny Eliza and, whenever she got into a passion, became much concerned for the salvation of her soul.

He used to go through books and carefully blot out any places where there was a frivolous mention of the Deity.

On a winter afternoon when he was four years and five months old he went to give his bread-pudding to an unfortunate widow.

As he was returning home a great black cloud came up and large hailstones fell in profusion.

That night he had a sore throat, which by morning had turned into a fatal illness.

His last words were 'God loves me and has pardoned all my sins. I am happy!' before he fell back pale and still and dead.

Henry Clump's little body turned to dust in the grave, but his soul went up to God.

## THE SINKING SPELL

*Edward Gorey/1963*

*O look, there's something way up high:*
*A creature floating in the sky.*

*It is not merely sitting there,*
*But falling slowly through the air.*

*The clouds grew pink and gold; its knees*
*Were level with the evening trees.*

*Morose, inflexible, aloof,*
*It hovered just above the roof.*

*It's gone right through, and come to rest
On great grand-uncle Ogdred's chest.*

*It settled further in the night,
And gave the maid an awful fright.*

*Head first, without a look or word,
It's left the fourth floor for the third.*

*The weeks went by; it made its way
A little lower every day.*

Each time one thought it might have stopped
One found, however, it had dropped.

One wonders just what can be meant
By this implacable descent.

It did not linger, after all,
Forever in the upstairs hall.

It found the drawing room in turn,
And slipped inside the Chinese urn.

*It now declines in fretful curves*
*Among the pickles and preserves.*

*It's gone beneath the cellar floor;*
*We shall not see it any more.*

A Future Unremembered Poet of the Seventeenth Century accepts a Christmas Cookie from the Great Veiled Bear

Edward Gorey/1980

**IS IT FUNNY?**

*Edward Koren/1978*

Like Grandville, whose menagerie of anthropomorphic mammals, fish, and fowl acutely characterized the mannerisms of the mid-nineteenth-century French bourgeoisie, Ed Koren's scruffy beasts and hirsute beings embody the idiosyncrasies of the urbane middle class. Like his predecessors at *The New Yorker*—Gluyas Williams and Peter Arno, whose caricatures incisively targeted the social types of the twenties and thirties—Koren's subhuman and more-human creatures exemplify the absurd mores and styles of the Bloomingdale's generation. Humor is, most of all, the means for Koren to dissipate anger. He places the unappealing aspects of society at bay, thereby creating the needed distance to make insightful, rather than vitriolic, comic criticism. Most significantly, he is a natural satiric draftsman whose scratchy pen line readily activates the funny bone, regardless of the subject, and whether or not it is accompanied by a caption.

A combination of many personal and artistic inspirations, Koren's drawing style evolved gradually. He was markedly influenced by Jimmy Hatlow ("A Tip of the Hatlow Hat" in the *New York World Telegram and Sun*), whose motion-charged drawings relied on crazy ideas and notions sent in by his audience. Al Capp's Shmoo, Sam Cobean's dogs, and James Thurber's beasts aided Koren in later developing his own prehistoric zoo. His subject matter derives from real life: "People never let me down," he says; "someone is always saying or doing something that makes me laugh." He translates these observations into images in which his sense of irony is supreme. A trip to Paris, early in his development as a cartoonist, afforded him an invaluable perspective on American behavior. Seeing the distinction between the two cultures allowed him to view the United States, especially New York, in a more analytical manner. He became a sort of "armchair sociologist." Able to experience and at the same time stand back from an event, he gathers fodder for his cartoon cannon.

Koren's satire masterfully blends a strong persona with a commentator's detachment: "When you are too involved with a subject, it can be dreary. My work is very remote from me, yet it is still mine." Unlike some comedians who portray themselves as schleps, Koren refuses to prey on himself or his condition as the basis of his humor. "I sometimes wonder where my tragic feelings are hiding, but even though I don't use myself, per se, in the drawings, they are still there." Sometimes he does indeed feel limited by the cartoon format: "There are deeper, darker feelings I cannot do in a cartoon. If you have a big, fat juicy metaphor, it works better in a larger noncartoon"—a thunderstorm, of sorts, instead of a shower. He employs his bestiary as a way of keeping further distance from his subjects. In a general sense, they are caricatures of his "everyman." Perhaps even more important, however, they are fun to draw.

Koren's work evidences two passions: his excitement about the act of drawing and his love of language. "I'm always surprised by what emerges from a drawing. In a very real sense I have no control. Sometimes some fantastic combinations occur—collisions of things you just don't expect." The best work happens when he draws without forethought or plan. He finds it much easier to freely associate on paper than in speech. Each of Koren's cartoons has its own sensibility and life: "If there is a point of view, it is in the craft. I do not resort to 'this is what I want to say,' because I'm not sure what I want to say." He admits to being terrified about doing a finish after the rough, afraid that he will lose the all important spontaneity. He is also aware of the intense political force inherent in a particular drawing, and so he chooses to make his graphic "attacks" more indirect. This subtle guise is what makes his satires so compelling, and, as he admits, "The people I satirize rarely see themselves as themselves." But we all know who they are.

**LESIURE HOURS ON THE PIKE**

*Edward Koren/1976*

**OUR VITAL LITERARY LIFE**

*Edward Koren/1977*

**LA CHASSE**

*Edward Koren/1975*

**OFFICER OF THE PEACE**
*Edward Koren/1974*

**STILL LIFE WITH FISH**
*Edward Koren/1974*

**RANKING MEMBERS**

*Edward Koren/1974*

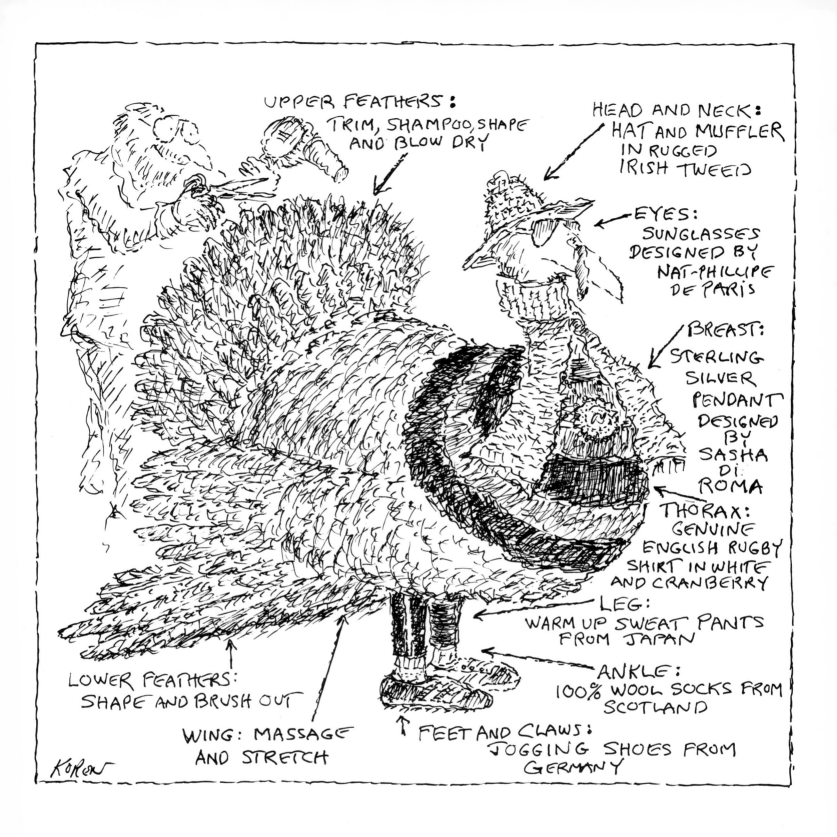

**A HOLIDAY RECIPE FOR PUTTING ON THE BIRD**

*Edward Koren/1976*

Bill Lee is a connoisseur of the absurd and a maven for burlesque comedy. An "investigative cartoonist" by vocation, he seeks out folly where no humorist has dared to journey and reports on the customs and mores of alien cultures. His search for the perfect cartoon "feature" has taken him to China, Russia, Hollywood, and Plains, Georgia—as well as to political conventions, movie sets, and countless neighborhood bars. His ribald muckraking, exposés of the world's leading blowhards and foes, such as Idi Amin and the Moral Majority, are always occasions for hearty laughter. His pictures remind us that ridicule is a good weapon in the war against hypocrisy. Not all his cartoons are produced with pen and ink—clay is also a successful material in his repertoire. His most popular comic sculpture, a shrunken head of Nixon, is a powerful caricature that savagely captures the essence of the former president. For Lee there are no sacred cows, just fat cats and bleached whales—all potential targets of attack and fun.

Lee was born in Williamsburg, Brooklyn, whence comes a certain homespun humor, an enjoyment of movies, and a passion for puns. He was a photographer in the Army, then began his drawing career in the early sixties. He was schooled by R.O. Blechman (who taught a class at the School of Visual Arts) on the value of the rendered line. Unlike the styles of many of his contemporaries, Lee's manner of drawing was unencumbered by an excess of tonal washes and sketchy pen strokes. Rather, he employed a clean, curvilinear approach that allowed for amusing characterizations. Although true to the philosophical traditions of the comic establishment, Lee's style and content were a departure from the established, sophisticated mode of *The New Yorker*. He sold cartoons to the major gag markets, including the *Saturday Evening Post, Cosmopolitan, Playboy, Evergreen Review*—the first American journal to display a decidedly European sensibility—allowed Lee's associative wit a chance to flourish. A wonderful example of his ironic playfulness was a Christmas cover for *Evergreen* in which Santa Claus lies face down in the snow, while two perplexed police officers, smoking guns in hand, stand over the body.

Lee enjoys playing with different forms. He experimented with two comic strips through which he exposed his innermost obsessions: in "Alexander the Great," he paid homage to his ideal heroic champion, and in "Americarnal," he indulged his sexual fantasies, political biases, and anticlerical beliefs on a weekly basis for the underground press. "Crucifixations"—a comic look at the birth of Christianity—is his most infamous series. Although these cartoons were amusing to many viewers, the printers hired to produce them found the blasphemy in the work beyond redemption and refused to run the presses. They were finally published by the less-outraged night shift. For Lee, this occurrence was a commonplace nuisance since irreverence is an integral part of his work. Lee, however, can also be a gentle commentator. His once-syndicated cartoon "Fogarty" (named for the mythical bartender and owner of a small bar and grill located somewhere in Queens, New York) was a delightful world of everyday people, each with their own special idiosyncrasies.

Lee is constantly drawing. His spaghettilike lines fill countless sketchbooks with scenes, people, and still lifes. His continuing development as a humorist rests on two important priorities: his concern for the problems of society and the desire to expand his own artistic limits. His mastery, for instance, of an expressionist color sense has recently surfaced. This is, in part, thanks to the fluidity of the studio marker, which he wields like a paintbrush. Also, as humor editor of *Penthouse* magazine, he is afforded the means to express himself in vibrant process colors and hues—color being at a premium in most American cartoon outlets. The combination of intense personal loves and hates, both aesthetic and worldly, make Lee a compelling satirist and a funny man.

"*Follow that Cab!*"

*Bill Lee/1976*

Bill Lee/1977

1.

2.

*Bill Lee/1978*

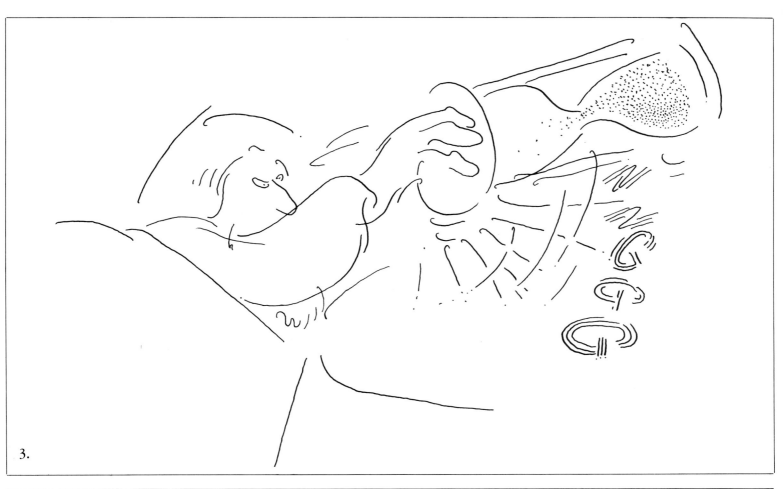

3.

4.

Bill Lee/1975

"Oops!"

Bill Lee/1974

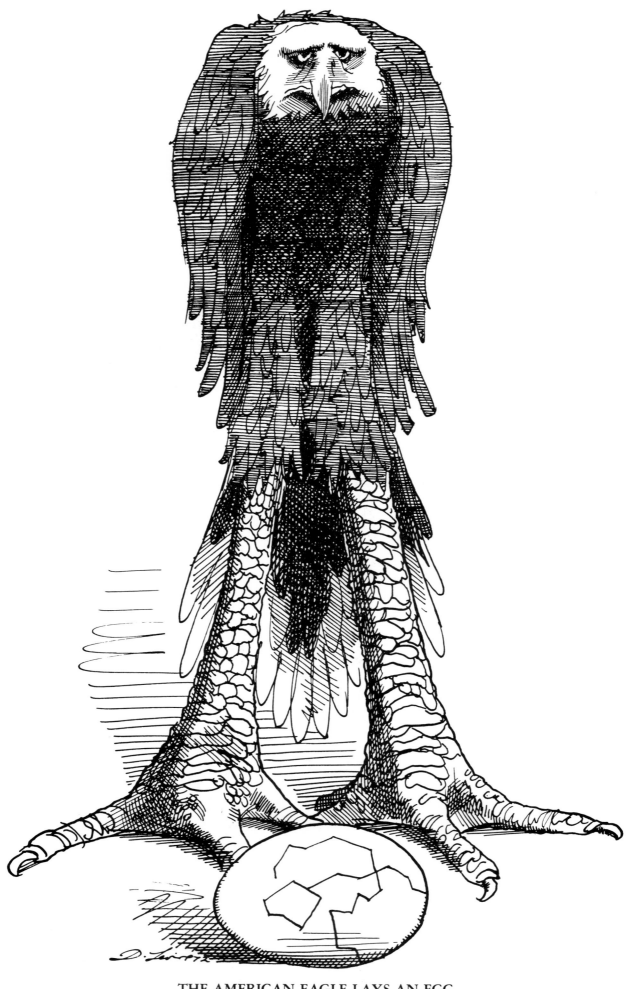

**THE AMERICAN EAGLE LAYS AN EGG**

*David Levine/1972*

If imitation is the ultimate form of praise, then David Levine has certainly been honored thousands of times by the countless cartoonists all over the globe whose styles are line-for-line replicas of his own. This is not surprising since it was Levine who revived the potent nineteenth-century art of political caricature, an art once brilliantly practiced by Daumier, Gill, Tenniel, Keppler, and Nast, and long supplanted in this century by Art Nouveau and Deco caricature. Further, his irreverent portraits appealed to the first generation in decades that refused to blindly accept the ideology and policy (specifically with regard to the Vietnam War) of political leaders. It was a generation in need of some concrete rallying point and Levine offered that focus by articulating a point of view which attacked, with fervent humor, those in power. And because of the mannered elegance of his drawing, unique at that time, he also fostered a renaissance in the field of newspaper cartooning.

Levine had been markedly influenced by all the comic arts—animation and comic books (especially Will Eisner's "Spirit") as well as Rembrandt's "caricatures." At Tyler Art School in Philadelphia he was introduced to the traditions of Realist painting (he is today an accomplished watercolorist and painter) and was delighted to find cartoon elements in Mannerist and Expressionist canvases. Although he graduated as a painter, he continued to do cartooning for fun—it also allowed him to move further into a modern idiom. "A radical unfactionalized socialist," he did his early cartoons for the *Daily Worker.* He then went into a failing Christmas card business, where he created drawings in the manner of the nineteenth-century *Punch* artist Richard Doyle: This work was noticed by Clay Felker, then a feature editor at *Esquire,* who offered Levine the opportunity to do a monthly spot drawing. When he couldn't come up with an idea to illustrate the accompanying text, he would draw someone prominent in the arts. The large head and little body (a convention that later became his trademark) fit perfectly into the small space. The *New York Review of Books* subsequently offered him not only unlimited space in their pages but also the license to do as he pleased. He has been exhibiting there ever since.

Levine's virtuosity is evidenced in his beautifully modeled caricatures of both vintage and contemporary artists, scientists, statesmen, and (most prolifically) literary figures. Unlike other renderings of this kind, derived from photographs and historical prints, Levine's *portraits* are critical studies rather than graphic redundancies. His distinctive linear approach—the tight cross-hatchings of the face and the economy of the body—have a peculiar kinship to the pantomimes of Charlie Chaplin. Like Chaplin, Levine's impact depends on the rendering of motion, expression and subtle detail. By extension, just as run-of-the-mill slapstick rarely has a lasting impact on an audience, a neophyte cartoonist who employs its graphic equivalent and simply collages a big head on a small body—ignoring the sensitivity inherent in a Levine drawing—will never make a poignant statement.

Unlike many of the daily editorial cartoonists who are out to amuse rather than edify their audience, Levine is firm in his conviction that cartoon commentary must be strengthened by commitment: "I've always had a political bias. I see the role of a political cartoonist is to attack power. I don't stand in awe of political positions. They are just human beings with a little more corruption. Many cartoonists have no sense that politicians are the enemy, especially when they rush a country into war. With that understanding I am able to do stronger work. I will always go after the administration as harshly as I can." Art, however, is not usually the leader, and Levine sees his role as a cartoonist as one who merely confirms the beliefs of those who hold similar views.

Cartoonists must maintain an adversary relationship with politicians. Often this necessary tension is placed on tenuous ground when the victim cheerily calls the cartoonist, hoping to purchase a particular work. On a few occasions Levine has been asked to sell a drawing to the very subject of his ire. One time a legislator made such a request and was told that he would have to pay a hefty sum. His response was predictable: "That's a hell of a price to ask a U.S. Senator."

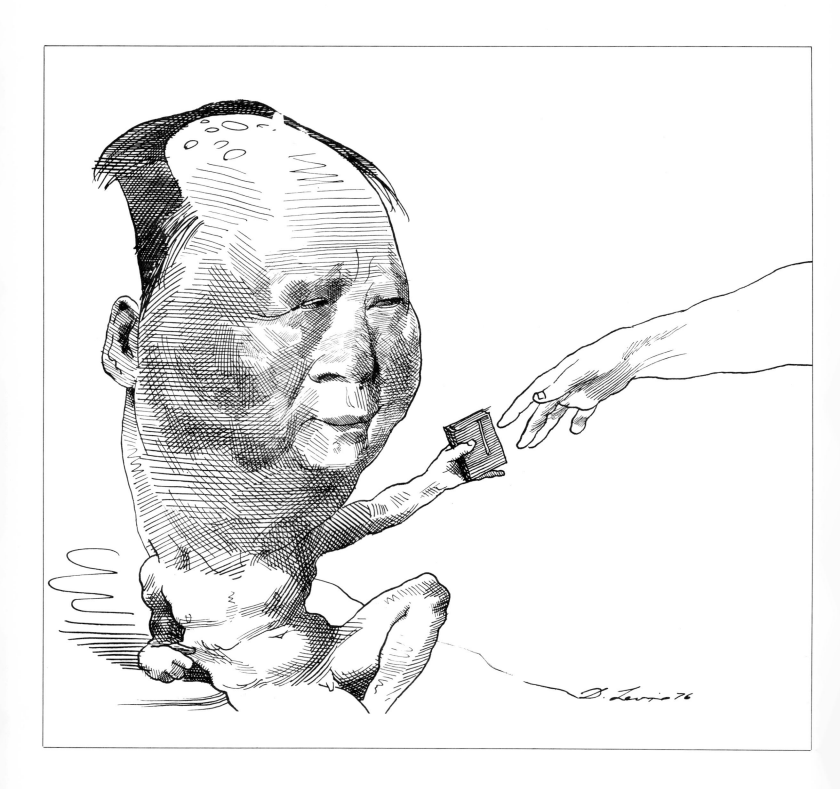

**MAO**

*David Levine/1976*

**LYNDON AND DEAN**

*David Levine/1967*

**MUSSOLINI**

*David Levine/1974*

**BERNINI'S ST. THERESA**

*David Levine/1971*

**RICHARD NIXON**

*David Levine/1973*

**CRUSADER POPES**

*David Levine/1970*

**THE ILLUSTRATED MAN**
*David Levine/1980*

**GODFATHER**
*David Levine/1972*

Marcel Mercier, of Reno, Nevada, a French-born swimming teacher, was discovered in Monte Carlo by a rich elderly American lady who brought him to Tampa, Florida and married him.
After her death in 1958 he opened his first night-club in Florida, "Crazy Doody." This was the beginning of the famous chain of night-clubs.
Mercier was married several times and his present wife is the delicious young busty blonde, Nanette Webster, Miss Nebraska of 1973.
He has a number of children but rarely speaks of them: "I'm not very interested in children, they take too much time. I'd rather make money and enjoy life," he says with his sexy French accent and his smile that few can resist.
He gave his very important collection of erotic art to the Reno Art Center.

*Pierre Le-Tan/1979*

114

# Pierre Le-Tan

Most cartoonists derive themes from external stimuli, which are then translated into personal terms. The subconscious is too limited a resource for artists in need of communicating ideas. Even Steinberg's Joycean satires arise from and comment upon universally held perceptions of time, space, and language. Pierre Le-Tan, however, rejects this notion; he is responsive more to his fantasies than to his environment. His lighthearted comic strips emerge full blown from his wonderfully fluid, yet disciplined, imagination—and in this sense he owes more to Art Brut than to the realist tradition in which he participates. His drawings are celebrations of form and fancy that bridge the gap between cartoon and illustration. His facile style is unburdened by the conventions of either genre. Unlike others in this volume, his innocent approach does not disguise issues of great significance. Le-Tan's drawings are not weapons at all, and what bite they have is not directed at any concrete foe. His flights of fancy simply reflect his unusual comic obsessions.

Whether or not his images are created on assignment, they display an enjoyment of the surreal idiom and the irony derived from juxtaposing the material with the imagined. He is at ease drawing a menagerie of anthropomorphized beasts for a children's book or replicating a lemon, a corkscrew, and a dish in mysterious repose, for the cover of *The New Yorker*. He can make a detailed portrait on commission as effortlessly as he can conjure up the absurd visage of some fictionalized character. Le-Tan's cartoon panels and sardonic narratives are personal comments done for his own amusement—and for the appreciation of others.

Le-Tan was born and raised in Paris. He attended L'Ecole des Arts Décoratifs, but lost interest in the curriculum after three months. His father is a professional painter and so Le-Tan began drawing at an early age. "I always drew in the same way," he recalls, "except my drawings were less elaborate then and perhaps not as good." He developed an ardent love of museums—and later a passion for the paintings and literature of the Bloomsbury group, especially Roger Fry and Vanessa Bell. Many late-nineteenth-century landscape paintings, as well as the detailed decorative works of Rex Whistler, among others, adorn his studio walls. He is an admirer of Steinberg and David Hockney, and like them Le-Tan is passionate about detail. In 1968, while he was still in school, he began to sell "spots"—drawings of windows, urns, chairs, and interiors—to *The New Yorker*. A year later they bought his first cover design. About his drawings he states: "I love to render with simplicity." His deadpan characters are both primitive and sophisticated at the same time. "Often I just draw what is in front of me but I add a little something extra. I've always enjoyed life drawing, especially faces, but most of the funny people come from my head." He is proficient with the cross-hatched line and with water color, and is happy to jump back and forth between the two.

Given the precision of his work, he produces at a prodigious rate. Although he is not a humorist by design, many of his drawings exhibit a typically French comic spirit. When *Horizon* magazine offered lavish portfolio space to individual artists, Le-Tan was asked to submit. He developed a fictional rogues' gallery of tycoons: "They were not based on anyone specific. I did them simply because the rich are fun to look at." He is moving further in the direction of the graphic novella as the best means for telling tales: "I prefer the story form because it is more complete than other means available." Currently he is working on two projects that illustrate a dichotomy in his work. One, a novel of fantasy, about a painter in search of the ideal model for his perfect allegory; the travails of his odyssey ultimately end in paradox. The second is a plunge into the real world. A graphic essay on a peculiar segment of the French upper class, and their barroom haunts in Paris and on the Riviera. No doubt his characterizations will be rendered with grace and wit, for Le-Tan is a gentle comedian.

# ECCENTRICS OF THE WORLD

Lesley Banel loved to dress as a fruit.

Felix Bernstein walked about with a suitcase full of stones.

Wanda del Vault only talked to eggs.

Romano Tong went everywhere in a motorized shoe.

The very rich and elegant Laura Wilton never combed her hair.

Wilbur Tucket lived in a tombstone.

*Pierre Le-Tan/1977*

Georges Mercier fed his paintings.

Toko Yumashi never looked at his feet.

Snooky Desvallières wrote giant letters to his friends.

Titi Kedriakis liked to be taken for a baby.

Rudolf Panov didn't wear ties.

Jo Draper loved eccentrics.

# DAPHNÉ BERG

A story by

Daphné Berg loved animals from the time she was a small girl.

Later they became her reason for living.

Since she was very rich, she could indulge her passion.

She lived in an enormous mansion with all her friends, and everybody had his own room.

Each one had what he liked. Paul preferred Louis XV furniture.

Roger loved plants.

*Pierre Le-Tan/1975*

# AND HER ANIMALS

Raoul liked to read.

Cynthia needed luxury.

Sometimes they would go out for long walks.

At night they would watch television.

Alas! One day Daphné lost everything.

Everyone was hungry; they ate her. She was good.

# LOU DEL BOCK.  A story by

Lou Del Bock was rich and hand-some.

Life had been good to him.

He was very successful with women.

His dogs loved him.

His swimming-pool was enormous.

*Pierre Le-Tan/1976*

# A PORTRAIT

Pierre Le-Tan

His collection of paintings was known throughout the world.

He took fabulous trips.

He even had his statue in a suburb of Detroit.

Often he gave fantastic parties; masked or fancy-dress balls.

Rich, he knew how to be generous.

He could have been blasé; but he had kept the soul of a child.

**THE FACE LIFT**
*Eugene Mihaesco/1979*

## Eugene Mihaesco

Surrealism in comic art is definitely a European phenomenon. The bizarre cartoons of the nineteenth-century fantasists Grandville and Robida influenced various aspects of the twentieth-century avant-garde, and afforded Dada and Surrealist practitioners the foundation on which to build a modern visual vocabulary. Before their satiric anti-art philosophy was absorbed into the mainstream of culture, these artists engaged in happenings designed to foment dissent—and at times rebellion. Although their revolution was never realized, they did bequeath to subsequent generations an aesthetic spirit that has noticeably affected the style of contemporary satiric illustration. Eugene Mihaesco is a preeminent recipient of the modernist sensibility expounded by Max Ernst, Paul Klee, and Marcel Duchamp. His work embodies elements of the past—specifically an engraving manner and Victorian symbology—time-machined into the present as tools with which to comment on topical issues. Mihaesco's graphic lyricism is a foil for the pointed irony of his statements, and the vigor of his message is rarely lost when it is focused on issues such as human rights. Mihaesco's command of pen and ink makes him a formidable artist; his European sense of the comic produces unique cartoons.

Mihaesco was born in Rumania, the birthplace of Tristan Tzara, Eugene Ionesco, Saul Steinberg (a supreme influence), and André François. He derives from his homeland a sensitivity to and an appreciation of the ridiculous: "Rumania is truly a Dada country," he says. "The absurd is everywhere represented in language, writing, and art." (Rumania is, as Steinberg has depicted it, one big cartoon.) He advanced his design ability while schooling in Bucharest, where he developed an intimate knowledge of art history and a virtuosic handling of color. He acquired an intense hatred both for the ruling powers, who restricted artistic expression, and for bureaucracy. As soon as he was able, Mihaesco emigrated to Lausanne, Switzerland—the base from which he now travels to Paris and New York. His critical persona emerged on the pages of *La Figaro* and, most significantly, on the Op-Ed page of the *New York Times*, where he successfully married his finely tuned aesthetics to the illustration mode. What resulted were drawings that commented on rather than literally illustrated a text or idea. In fact, the manuscript (which he prefers to work from) merely became the occasion for graphic articulation of important concerns. He manufactured his own lexicon of images, made from bits and pieces of Sears Roebuck catalogues, *fin de siècle* ephemera, and, sometimes, borrowings from other artists held in esteem. His drawings have the ambiance of a thrift shop, without the clutter. Collagelike, they include diverse elements (feathers, irons, keys, swords, timepieces) which are juxtaposed in order to create a sense of mystery. The comic and absurd are always apparent in these well-rendered, linear tableaux, as they are in his more sketchy spot drawings as well. His work is basically poetic—hidden meaning and double entendre abound. Although he gives titles to many of the pieces, the words are incidental—the humor of drawing is what shines.

Mihaesco's color work is markedly different from his black-and-white. It covers the spectrum from subtle pastels to vibrant primaries (most apparent in his collages). These pieces speak of a personal aesthetic sensibility; their content is, on the whole, more whimsical. His *New Yorker* covers are homages to the city he loves, while his collages often satirize artistic trends that have markedly affected his own development.

The satiric impulse is apparent in all of Mihaesco's work, but not all of his work is satiric. He can attack a particular foe—most prolifically, the Soviet Union—or gently reflect on one of life's many paradoxes he witnesses while walking around New York. If the subject calls for it, Mihaesco can be sardonic, but foremost, it seems, he enjoys being visually playful.

**THE CAT**

*Eugene Mihaesco/1980*

**WINDING UP**

*Eugene Mihaesco/1979*

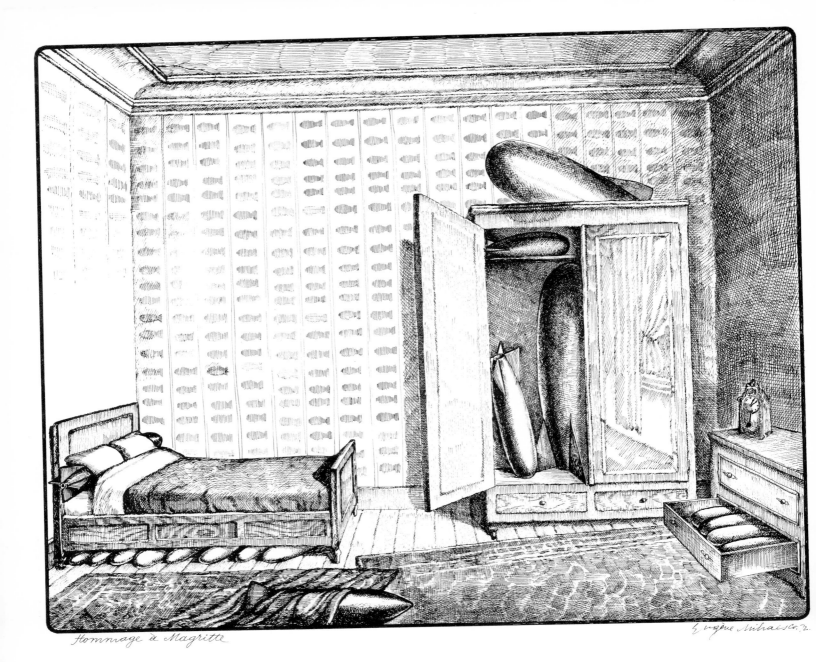

Hommage à Magritte

Eugene Mihaesco. 73.

**ROOM WITH A VIEW**

*Eugene Mihaesco/1973*

**TRISTAN TZARA'S WATCH**

*Eugene Mihaesco/1979*

**REVENGE**

*Eugene Mihaesco/1980*

**DADA COUNTRY**
*Eugene Mihaesco/1977*

Lou Myers/1978

# Lou Myers

What do the following have in common?: anthropocentrism, Arabs, armament, big business, Catholicism, consumerism, corruption, duplicity, economics, flashers, matinée day, militarism, MX missiles, mother, money, narcissism, politics, pornography, perverts, psychiatry, Richard Nixon, sex, television, Times Square, violence, Vietnam, women's lib, and the pursuit of happiness. The answer: all have been integrated and often lacerated in Lou Myers' cartoons.

For thirty years he has craftily lampooned our worldly and spiritual excesses in drawings that exhibit the unhampered freedom of a child's fingerpainting. In actuality this blotchy linear approach is an expressive calligraphy that transforms the boisterous, opinionated Myers persona into concise, emphatic visual statements. Myers has liberated his graphic form from the burdens of the gag line. His drawings are action-filled pantomimes which often succeed, where most others fail, at combining slapstick with intelligence. He has harnessed the magic of the comic by utilizing an important characteristic of visual comedy: the tension between man and machine. Looking at a Myers drawing, one marvels at the ease with which those starkly rigid characters are able to gesture.

Lou Myers was born in Paris and grew up in East Harlem, New York, during the twenties. His first political cartoons appeared before the war in the rabidly antifascist *New Masses*. During the war he worked as a U.S. Navy portrait painter of ranking officers and later served as a combat artist during the Rhine Valley crossing. His first illustration work included posters for Columbia Pictures and two books, *Strange Scenes at the Zoo* and *Clemeta*—"I did the best crowd scenes ever in those books." He returned to Paris in the early fifties and illustrated a book by Art Buchwald. He soon produced weekly satiric drawings that appeared on the back page of *Paris-Match*, entitled "Sans Parole" (Without Caption). The magazine sent him as a graphic reporter to Rome, where his already unique graphic approach derived a European comic sensibility. Of his simple graphic style he says: "If I could finish a drawing fast, I could go to the theater, read a book, or visit a museum—instead of being saddled by boring technique." Back in the United States he was staff scribbler for *Monocle* and created a cartoon character named Boris Yudkin: "It was the best thing I did then. It went on for pages. He was a Russian seducer who used American products—hair spray, dishwashing liquid—as a leitmotiv for getting women into bed."

Myers is a voracious reader on all subjects—fuel for future satiric fires. Many of his pet peeves, however, derive from more visceral stimuli in close proximity to the heart. Numerous cartoons are aimed at members of the psychiatric community: "They are the enemy," he says. "Before psychoanalysis, a comic or tragic play would help man to see his foolishness—a Greek concept. Now all the fools remain idiots because these psychiatrists merely adjust people to the system. Sometimes it's better to be radicalized." Of television, another recurring theme, he says: "When TV is bad, it is an abomination. It is a perfect medium for the dictator; it blinds people into accepting evil as theater." He has done drawings for all the major cartoon outlets, often running up against the predictable censorship imposed on an outspoken humorist. However, Myers' comedy has never suffered because of editorial pressures. In fact, it has been strengthened.

In the tradition of Alexander King, James Thurber, and S.J. Perelman, Myers is an accomplished short-story writer. The majority of his pieces, for *The New Yorker,* have been about his mother's life in the Workman's Circle nursing home: "When I started to go there, my mother was not completely stoned out. She would fill my head with her own crazy world. I found the home was a bedlam of lunacy—it was fascinating. I got to know other interesting women as well and began to write it down." Whether it is in a cartoon, a story, a lecture, or a conversation on the phone, Myers brings the world's lunacy into necessary focus.

**THE ADMAN**

*Lou Myers/1977*

"Rogers go in for Kaplan."

Lou Myers/1974

Here's the ad-idiot who did the 'I smell clean' ads on TV...

...and that 'Don't squeeze the Charmin' ads...

...and that damned 'Aunt Blue Belle here'...

...and 'Ring around the collar.'

...also that unbelievable Rudi the delicatessen man in the 'Hansel and Gretel' cold cuts ads...

...and worst of all he wrote the 'Plop, plop, phiz, phiz—oh what a relief it is'

*Lou Myers/1977*

Agent X says Ivanoff
got microfilm, 1 of
each and 2 decoded
messages, but was shot dead
by security guards...
but not before he gave
her the secrets....
'without Ivanoff,' she says
'the world is upside down'
but, 'that's life' she says..

Loumyers

Lou Myers/1977

**NIXON**

*Robert Osborn/1970*

# Osborn

Having combined classical and expressionist approaches into highly energized, personal satiric statements, Robert Osborn is a pioneer of modern American cartooning. The foremost example of this is his book of drawings *War Is No Damn Good,* published immediately after World War II. This monograph is a milestone in the history of cartoon art, rekindling the critical tradition exemplified by Goya's *Disasters of War.* Not since George Grosz and Otto Dix created their visual prophecies of war and fascism three decades earlier had this mode been practiced. Further, the book marked a radical stylistic departure because of its unique draftsmanship—a blend of fast brushstrokes, large areas of flat color, and a linear simplicity that framed a mélange of insightful graphic symbols. This style became a major influence on the work of cartoonists for some time to follow. For the next thirty-five years Osborn continued to be a forceful political and social commentator as he attacked such issues as ecology and armament (before it became chic to do so) and such politicians as Joseph McCarthy (despite the threat of blacklisting).

Osborn was born in Oshkosh, Wisconsin. He was encouraged to draw by his mother, who supplied him with paints and brushes, and by his father, who gave him paper from the family paper mill. He was inspired by the comedy of Charlie Chaplin and Buster Keaton and influenced by the art of Peter Newell, Arthur Rackham, and Palmer Cox. He moved east to attend Yale, where he worked on the *Yale Record* with Peter Arno and Dwight MacDonald. In 1923, when Harold Ross was publishing the first issues of *The New Yorker,* he asked Osborn to submit some drawings. Although all but one of the sketches were rejected, the package of returned cartoons always contained lengthy critiques in the hope that there would be more acceptable submissions: "He tried to make me into a one-line cartoonist," recalls Osborn. Finally he submitted a cartoon showing a man leaping from a trapeze and missing the hands of his partner on the opposite bar. The caption read: "Oops, sorry." The idea was bought ($5.00 was the going rate), however, Ross hired someone else to do the rendering. Years later Osborn learned from James Thurber that Ross always pointed to that idea as the "perfect *New Yorker* gag—a masterpiece of simplicity." Even though *The New Yorker* style was not the right form for Osborn, he became passionate about the simple line as the ultimate means to articulate an idea. This was evident in the work of those artists he admired most—George Herriman, Ralph Barton, and F. G. Cooper. In 1928 he left for Europe for a two-year stay during which he looked at artistic riches by day and made drawings by night. When he returned to the States in 1930, he began to paint in the manner of Daumier. But he found that his art was nothing more than a rehash of other artists': "I kept hearing from critics, 'Hasn't so and so done this better?'" Osborn's graphic personality finally emerged in a sixteen-page letter written to a friend, recalling a recent hunting trip. It was jammed with watercolors. The recipient showed the letter to Tom Coward of Coward, McCann, who commissioned several books of drawings that were destined for success.

Osborn became politically aware at the time that Franklin Roosevelt became President. Unable, for health reasons, to join the Lincoln Brigade, he became an active member in an anti-fascist group and created drawings designed to influence public opinion in favor of aiding Britain. His drawings of this period, in the manner of other political cartoonists such as Louis Raemaekers, Rollin Kirby, and J.N. Darling, were self-assured commitments to the cause. In 1941 he enlisted in the Navy and was assigned to an office of information headed by Edward Steichen, where he created training manuals in comic-book form—classics today. By his own count, Osborn produced at least 30,000 drawings for the Navy. He says it is the main reason he acquired the flowing line.

After the war he contributed acerbic commentaries to *Harper's* and the *New Republic:* "I was given the freedom to draw what I felt. And when it is clearly felt, that's when the drawing succeeds." Over the next three decades he completed numerous books of graphic criticism including *On Leisure, The Vulgarians,* and *Missile Madness,* all dealing harshly and honestly with possible human disasters. And his art continues to grow. A few years ago, when Franco died, Osborn spent days trying to achieve just the right likeness of the dictator—to insure that his evil would not be forgotten. The result: a brilliant drawing—neither caricature nor portrait, just a few well-placed lines—in a class all its own.

**NOT EXACTLY COMPATIBLE**

*Robert Osborn/1960*

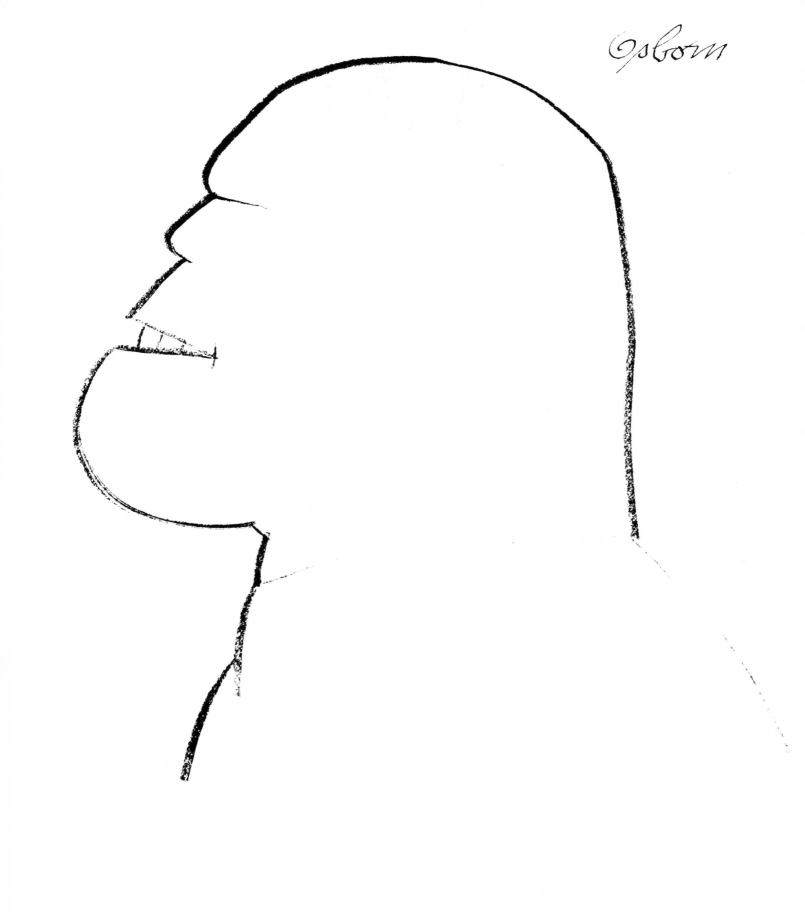

**MR. FORD**

*Robert Osborn/1976*

**MIRVING**

*Robert Osborn/1970*

**THE SENATOR**
*Robert Osborn/1965*

**RAMPANT INDECISION**

*Robert Osborn/1960*

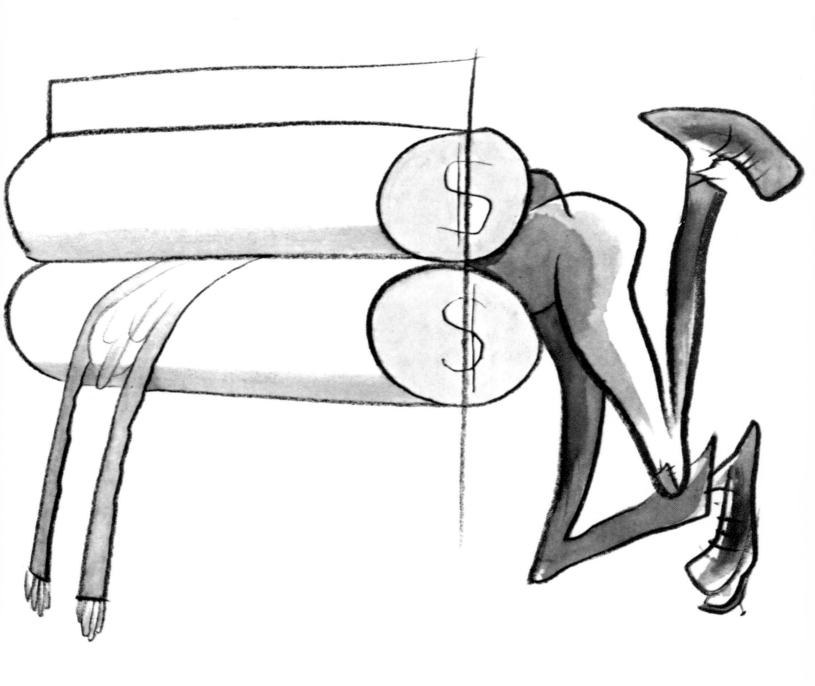

**TAXES**

*Robert Osborn/1960*

**THE RAT RACE**
*Robert Osborn/1960*

**SILLY PEOPLE**

*Hans Georg Rauch/1980*

Some cartoonists brilliantly articulate their points of view with a minimum of linear baggage, while others achieve their ends through the speedy application of random pen- and brushstrokes. Hans-Georg Rauch has successfully worked both ways in the past, but his current approach is distinctively more complex. In fact, he is one of the most ambitious draftsmen working in the cartoon genre. He employs an intricate engraving style in which baroque and modern architectural edifices and accouterments are arduously, yet magnificently, rendered. They serve as a counterpoint to the more economical, precise drawings of individuals and crowds which comprise his tableaux. Rauch's graphic virtuosity, however, should not be dwelt upon for too long, lest we ignore the conceptual strength of his work. These drawings are by no means examples of the all too common style-over-content malady suffered by compulsive artists whose attention to cosmetic detail has run amok. On the contrary, Rauch's cartoons are well-thought-out ideas depicting "man" as both the creator and the prisoner of the twentieth century's technological and philosophical legacy, the roots of which stem from the massive industrial rebirth which he lived through in his native West Germany.

Rauch was born in Berlin in 1939. He studied art in Hamburg and was later influenced by a stay in the south of France. His early cartoon work included sight gags rendered with characteristic elegance. He derived strength from Steinberg and Searle, but these affinities are obviously only a spiritual background for his unique approach to satire. His intimate knowledge of the history of print and of printmaking itself have afforded him the ability to create drawings in a similar mode. (He is also an accomplished etcher and has completed a series of extremely intricate aquatints.) A love of history in general provided the sources for visual reference. As a freelance illustrator he worked on commissions for countless French, German, Dutch, Belgian, and Swiss magazines. He was introduced to American audiences in *Look, Holiday, Lithopinion,* and, most significantly, the *New York Times,* where his personal graphic commentaries on the Op-Ed page were able to coexist with and not pander to the text (Vietnam, Watergate, and Detroit's big-car syndrome were among his concerns at this time). Numerous exhibitions both in the United States and Europe (most recently at the Wilhelm Busch Museum in Hannover) have afforded audiences a firsthand look at his technique. The published albums of his drawings evidence the range of his concerns—*Battlelines,* for example, is an ingenious look at the history of warfare as well as a reflection of his abhorrence of recent conflagrations.

Most cartoonists find that when their world view is too general, they fall into the deep pit of tired clichés. Not so for Rauch. It is true that his satiric targets include many grand monsters—the church, nuclear science, the military, prison, and world destruction—but his symbolic treatment transcends the familiar, and his humor and insight are attention-grabbing. He cleverly uses his personal vocabulary of architectural forms and cartoon figures to trap the viewer into a false sense of security (do not worry, dear audience, you won't be offended by imagery over one hundred years old) . . . and then, once in, he lowers the boom. His drawing concerning the reality of combat in this portfolio (page 157) is a seductive whisper that becomes a scream. Rauch's work is not concerned with aesthetics. Although a drawing may begin as a fixation with a particular graphic exercise—for instance, the innocent metamorphosis of a building or landscape into a fluid tapestry of armaments or garden of guns and bombs—the application of this imagery to the real world takes precedence.

In order to expand his horizons, Rauch has recently—with the aid of crayons, pencils, and watercolor—turned his attention to pigments other than black and white. The colored drawings in this portfolio are examples of a new comedic direction, subtle yet compelling. True to his previous work, these pictures camouflage the diabolical undertones of his commentary, perhaps setting the trap for future victims.

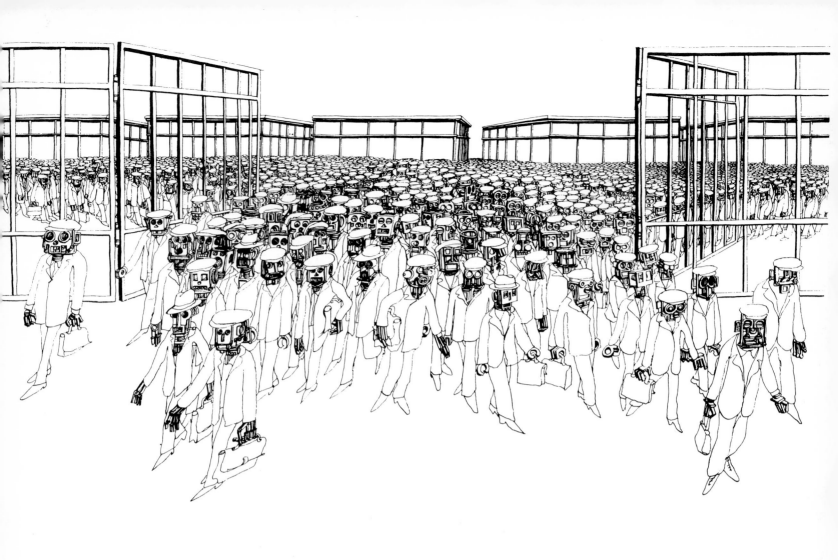

*Hans Georg Rauch/1973*

**BALANCE**

*Hans Georg Rauch/1974*

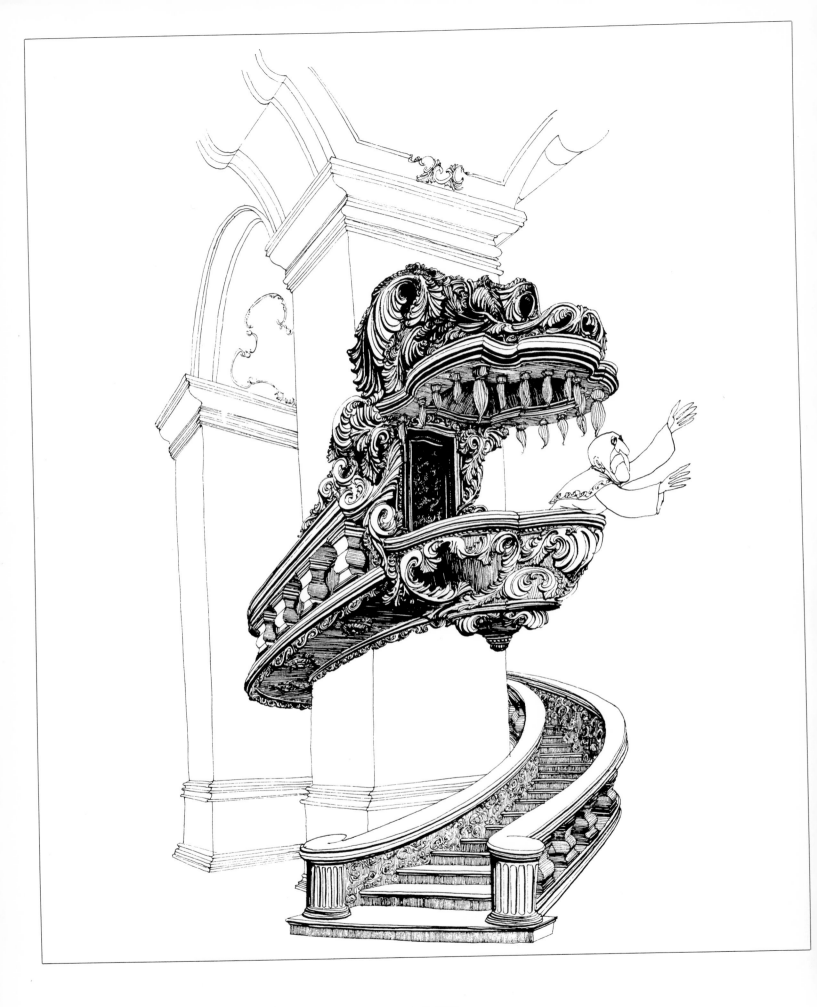

**THE LIE**

*Hans Georg Rauch/1975*

**"HI, HOW ARE YOU?"**

*Hans Georg Rauch/1980*

*Hans Georg Rauch/1974*

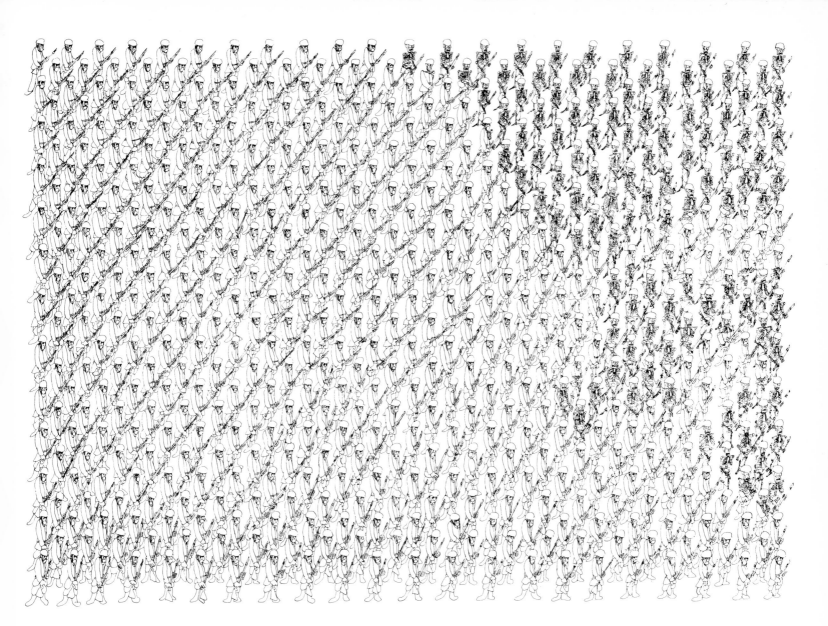

*Hans Georg Rauch/1975*

**THE MAN WHO LIKES TO TALK POLITICS**

*Arnold Roth/1977*

"The nineteen-fifties," says Arnold Roth, "were not as dull as people will tell you. There were the hips and nonhips, there was jazz, Mort Sahl, Lenny Bruce, and a lot of people fighting McCarthy and his various legislative clones." But all was not roses either. It was a period when the Senate investigations into the purity of cartoons fostered the Comics Code, a self-regulatory body of comic-book manufacturers who instituted a catechism of moral laws that effectively caused the death of America's most irreverent magazine, *Mad.* On the other hand, it was a time of publishing milestones: Hugh Hefner had success with *Playboy* and subsequently financed a new journal of farce, *Trump,* edited by *Mad's* guiding light, Harvey Kurtzman. Roth, then a young writer/cartoonist, was introduced to Kurtzman, who immediately put him on retainer. What resulted was an exciting collaboration in which satire flourished. Roth preferred sequential drawings and large-scale tableaux to the gag approach. His humor was directed at social phenomena: "Subjects like why people were using small cars interested me. We had Nixon then, too, you know. I felt that just baiting him in cartoons didn't tell much of a story. How we accepted a morally bankrupt leader like that was a more important issue to tackle." Roth's unique style evidenced a fascination with the baroque: "I loved Hogarth, Rowlandson, Gillray, and Cruikshank. In fact, I used to think of my sequences as small 'penny prints'."

Roth was born in Philadelphia in 1929. He attended the Philadelphia College of Art and began to do freelance illustration in 1952. His first drawings appeared in *TV Guide.* He did department headings for *Holiday* and record covers for West Coast jazz musicians such as Dave Brubeck. Roth freelanced for the John Hubley studio (along with Blechman, Crockett Johnson, and Gene Dietch), writing and drawing funny things relating to specific products that various advertising agencies were working on: "They were put into an idea bank for the account execs to refer to and use if necessary. It was about as interesting as advertising could be."

Next for Roth was *Trump,* which, unfortunately, folded before it hit the stands. "Hefner was put in a bind," he recalls. "*Colliers* magazine had folded and the banks, sensing a trend, called in his note. He either had to put a part of *Playboy* as collateral or fold *Trump.* He was very contrite about it since we all knew the magazine would have been successful." Roth then became a co-owner of *Humbug,* modeled after the old *Mad.* When that bit the dust, he moved on to *Help* (produced by Kurtzman, Terry Gilliam, and Gloria Steinem), which sent him on assignments to Moscow and Berlin as a satiric reporter. He developed a successful comic strip, "Poor Arnold's Almanac," for the *Herald Tribune* syndicate, which lasted three years. He then began a long relationship with *Punch* in Britain. In 1965 he was asked by *Punch* to replace P.G. Wodehouse, then ninety years old, who was doing the report from America. "I sent in two of the funniest pages I had ever seen written, which they sent back in the next mail with a note that said, 'Draw it, you fool'." He has been doing single panels and strips for them ever since.

Roth prefers graphic variety to the rigors of the cliché-ridden editorial cartoon. In *Politiks* magazine he was afforded the space to create a large, independent statement (rarely seen these days in any of the remaining satiric outlets) in which he could devote as much of himself to the drawing as to the idea. His expressive needs are as much fulfilled in the illustrative mode as in the self-initiated strip. He enjoys working in a historical context: "In humor, history ties things together nicely." Two of his most exciting strips are twisted views of the past: "The History of Pornography" for the *National Lampoon* and a serialized "History of Sex" for *Playboy.* ("When asked how long this strip would run, I said as long as I had tuitions to pay. It came to fifteen chapters.")

Roth is not an iconoclast by any means: "I'm a crank; I never liked anyone who calls life to order. I will always find something I'd like to do that was not on their agenda." (In the sixties he was criticized by the left as being right-wing for his support of Hubert Humphrey.) He recently completed a drawing satirizing the fight between the biblical creationists and the Darwinians which typifies his sense of fair play: "The idea that they are fighting is funny to me. Neither view should be censored."

**PICASSO AT WORK**

*Arnold Roth/1978*

**LEONARDO AT WORK**

*Arnold Roth/1978*

# ARNOLD ROTH'S HISTORY of the NEXT TEN YEARS

## 1980

## 1981

## 1982

## 1983

## 1984

IT WILL BE DECIDED TO NOT HAVE 1984 AS EVERYONE HAS READ THE BOOK, SEEN THE MOVIE, OR BOTH, AND KNOWS HOW IT COMES OUT.

*Arnold Roth/1979*

**1985**

**1986**

**1987**

**1988**

**1989**

AT THE INSISTENCE
OF CRANKS AND
NEATNESS NUTS,
WE WILL HAVE
**1984**
AFTER ALL.

# WHO'S WHOM IN AMERICA

*Arnold Roth's Bald Faced Survey of the Polyglot Melting Pot*

*1,200 Religious Nuts*

*209,537,083 Irreligious Nuts*

*220,000,000 Minority Group Members*

*12,707,548 Amateur Soap Carvers*

*1 Professional Discus Hurler*

*700 Professors of Bagpiping*

*1,212,003 Unemployed Ph.Ds*

*50,307,405 Employed Ph.Ds*

*Arnold Roth/1979*

*4,751,311 Unemployed Poets*

*0 Employed Poets*

*4 Bagpipe Students*

*1 President*

*17,000,000 Politicians*

*18,000,000 Crooked Politicans*

*87.4 Million Illegal Immigrants*

1762: Little Wolfgang Amadeus Mozart finds out that he is being paid by the note.

*Arnold Roth/1979*

**THE REPUBLICAN NATIONAL COMMITTEE
MEETS TO CONSIDER A NEW PARTY SYMBOL**

*Arnold Roth/1977*

**THE ARRIVAL OF GOD**
*Ronald Searle/1972*

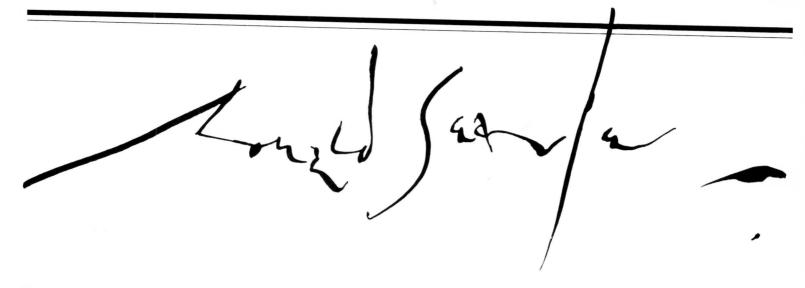

To thrust the laurels of "master" upon a contemporary artist is perhaps unfair and injudicious. Contemporary society seeks to feed its hunger for geniuses of all descriptions (and then often rejects them just as quickly). However, the truth is apparent in the case of Ronald Searle: he definitely is a formidable "master" of modern caricature. No other living cartoonist has taught and influenced so many followers as Searle has done over the past thirty years. His world prominence as a humorist, satirist, cartoonist, and author, was attained through his ability to blend nonsense and common sense into powerfully insightful comedies of human nature. He is a satiric magician, able, with a flick of the pen, to anthropomorphize the most unlikely beast into a reflection of man's foibles. His graphic travelogues (of Moscow, Las Vegas, Hollywood, and Berlin, among others) were insightful journeys into the heart of society, from which he drew upon the eccentricities of people and places heretofore obscured by postcard images. Searle has given his viewers so much of his soul—from joyful entertainments to humanist statements filled with humor and pathos. Even his solemn visual reportage (commissioned by the United Nations) of Adolf Eichmann's trial in Jerusalem did not pander to the commonplace. Rather, it afforded a fascinating account of a frightening spectacle. Although there are legions of cartoonists who carry Searle's stylistic and conceptual torch, and appear on the editorial pages of countless newspapers, only he can create the definitive ambiance and characterizations. Only he can wield those baroque and rococo lines—intricately or simply—making the comic such an integral part of our lives.

Ronald Searle was born in 1920 in Cambridge, England. Of his impulse to become a cartoonist he says: "In the late thirties, things in general and politics in particular were no longer neatly divided into black and white, but blurred at the edges. University student life was colored with the necessity to have an opinion of events that were inexorably strutting towards the ungentlemanly. Those years, the tail end of the romantic conception of goodies and baddies, were underlined by those who went off poetically to fight Fascism hand to hand in the Spanish Civil War—and who remained there, to fertilize fields on the outskirts of Barcelona. Other students, like the Burgesses and the Macleans, were being bedded and perspicaciously recruited by the erudite Blunt, as future Russian agents. And around the corner, in the Cavendish laboratory, the atom had been finally chipped and battered through and the first shovels of earth turned over for the dead of Hiroshima....It was enough to make a teenager jumpy. On top of this, there was the irresistible impulse to draw. I cannot remember wanting to be anything else other than An Artist although I had no idea in which direction I should point."

When Searle was fifteen, the local paper took him on as a weekly cartoonist. There he learned to draw for reproduction. He was also the resident artist for *Granta*, a weekly university paper whose staff included many future scholars, editors, publishers, and poets. At the weekly editorial meetings, he says, "I rapidly learned that you cannot simply open your mouth; you have to say something—however crass. Consequently, commentating—or at least, appearing to have an opinion—was thrust on me, still dampish from the cradle. It was then only a question of acquiring experience with which to back it." Cambridge further offered enough architectural diversions to keep an artist busy for eons. It had many museums—the anatomical museum, the rich collection of Turner watercolors, William Blake and Thomas Rowlandson drawings, and a prestigious collection of illuminated manuscripts. "Inevitably something of this had to rub off onto me." An introduction to the work of George Grosz was further inspiration. "By 1939 the ground had been ploughed and seeded and I left home for the first time and went to war." He left at age nineteen and after an arduous imprisonment in a Japanese POW camp, he returned to England at the age of twenty-six. While incarcerated, he further developed his craft using implements made from whatever he could muster. His drawings of prisoners and captors made in secret later became the basis for his first major exhibition. This was, perhaps, the last time his art was ever that somber again.

**POLLUTION**
*Ronald Searle/1972*

**THE WALL, BERLIN**

*Ronald Searle/1963*

**THE FLIGHT**
*Ronald Searle/1978*

**C'EST LA VIE**
*Ronald Searle/1975*

**THE BABY SITTER**

*Ronald Searle/1976*

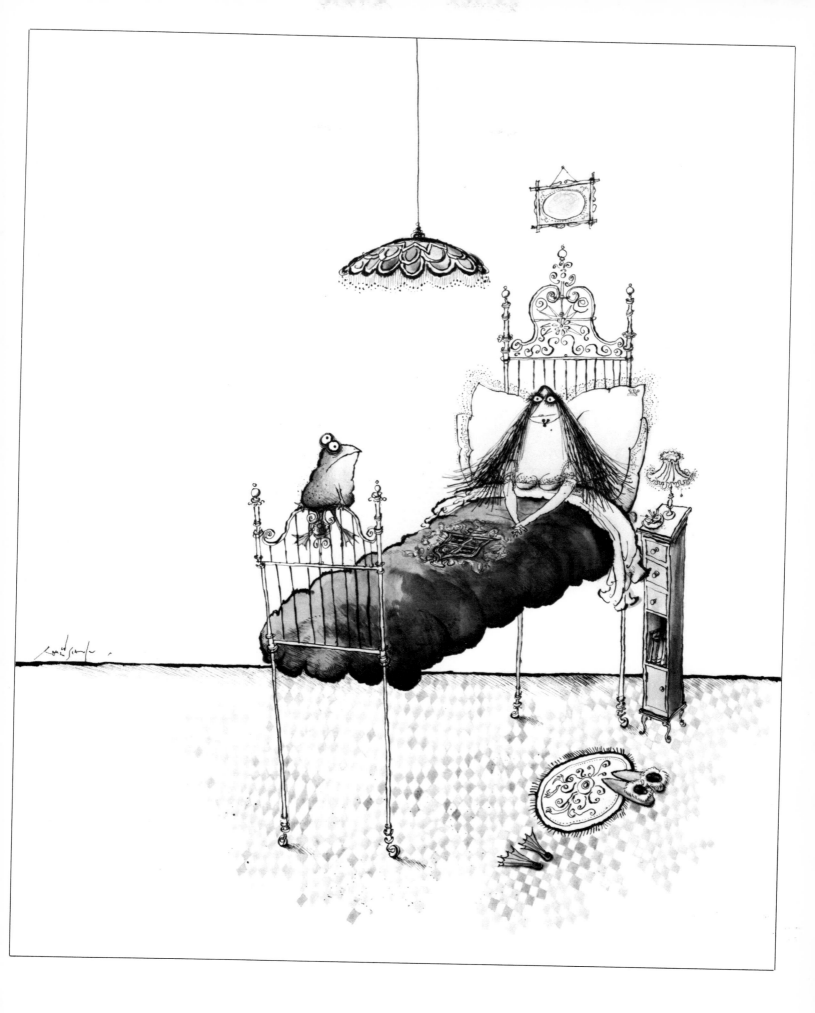

**THE FROG PRINCE**
*Ronald Searle/1975*

**YALTA**

*Ronald Searle/1967*

**THE SHRINE**
*Ronald Searle/1975*

*Jean-Jacques Sempé/1969*

# Sempé

Jean-Jacques Sempé's comic tableaux are delightfully French and acutely universal. Although his backdrops re-create Paris, Saint-Tropez, and the suburbs, and although his characters come from the bourgeois, petit bourgeois, and peasant classes, an appreciation of his drawings is not limited by geographical location. His comic vision is free from the yoke of unmanageable generalizations. His drawings are spotlights that shine on the quirks and nervous tics of all societies. His humor is directed at a world that is being consumed by a perverse taste for speed, economic status, and social regimentation. These cartoons are unhampered by ideology. Rather, they derive from an intimate relationship with his cultural surroundings. "When I draw a little man," he says, "crushed by his environment, it's not the Environment that's important, it's the ambiance." He refuses to be labeled or placed into either artistic or political pigeonholes. "I don't have any group spirit. I could never work on a team; I don't trust people who categorically impose their ideas or judgments." He has been lambasted by the left wing as establishment and cursed by the right as "communist." "Sometimes I will do a drawing with political overtones; I get letters from the right, left, and the center. I figure if all parties are offended, it's proof that no offense was intended." His satiric range is broad-based, emphasizing the more fashionable, modern aspects of society—art, architecture, manners, and, most significantly, language. "If I had the cultural facilities, I would study language more—because humor today springs out of the immense distance that exists between words and reality." Of Sempé's import as humorist, Ed Koren states, "He is much more psychologically penetrating than any cartoonist I know of. There is a wealth of complicated human feeling in his work. It is rich with subtle, observed interconnections."

Sempé was born in Bordeaux, France. He was an indifferent student with two passions, music and soccer, but he didn't excel in either. To console himself he started making drawings of athletes and musicians. He tested for all sorts of jobs—with Social Security, the National Railroad, various banks, the Postal Service. "Not one of these organizations saw in me the zealous employee I would have been. They didn't spot in my fantastic errors of addition and subtraction the temperament of the outstanding businessman that dwelled within me." So he went into illustration and lettering: "a little bit of everything." He subsequently joined the army and completed national service at a disciplinary barracks. "People thought I was a hothead and a dreamer. I was just acting according to my own logic." He kept up his drawing, and when he was discharged he began to sell to all the French newspapers. He also contributed to *Match* and *Punch*. His first album of drawings was published in Switzerland in 1957, and he has been doing albums ever since. A weekly cartoon in *L'Express* helped to sharpen his incisive wit.

Sempé sees himself as maladjusted, unable to keep pace with the trends of contemporary society. Although often accused of hating modern life, he feels that "Our life today is not modern enough. If I make a drawing of New York City covered in dirt and pollution, what I'm saying is not that I hate New York City, but that I hate dirt and pollution. For me, to be 'modern' means to simplify living—if it doesn't simplify, then it's not modern at all."

When asked about the future, Sempé replies: "More and more I want to do drawings where nothing happens, without gags, without justification. . . . It annoys me when people make false interpretations of my sketches, a definition that encloses me in a system each time." Sempé's most recent work, *The Musicians*, seven years in the making, is an homage to the music-makers, both real and fictional, who people his world. He has eliminated gag lines in favor of superbly crafted vignettes and sensitively characterized personages. "The facade of the musician is very different from the reality of his life. The interior life of the musician has much to do with the realm of solitude." With this album his artistic personality has reached a pinnacle—he has scored a unique graphic symphony with subtle rhythm and grace.

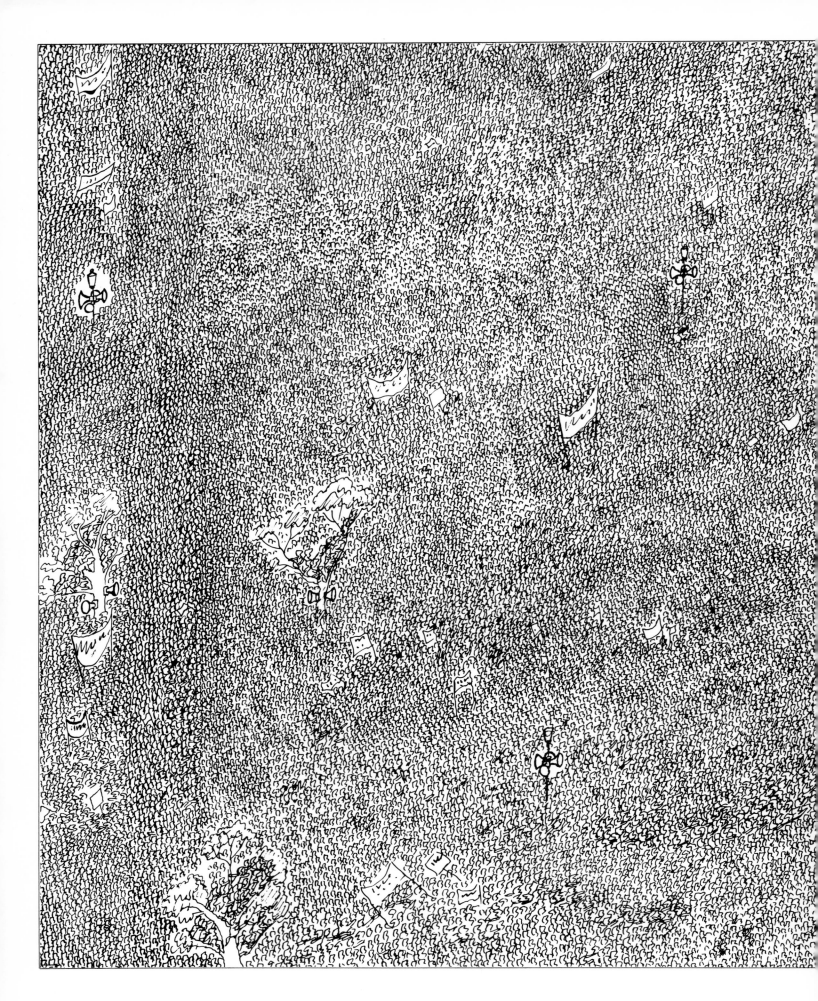

Jean-Jacques Sempé/1974

Jean-Jacques Sempé/1974

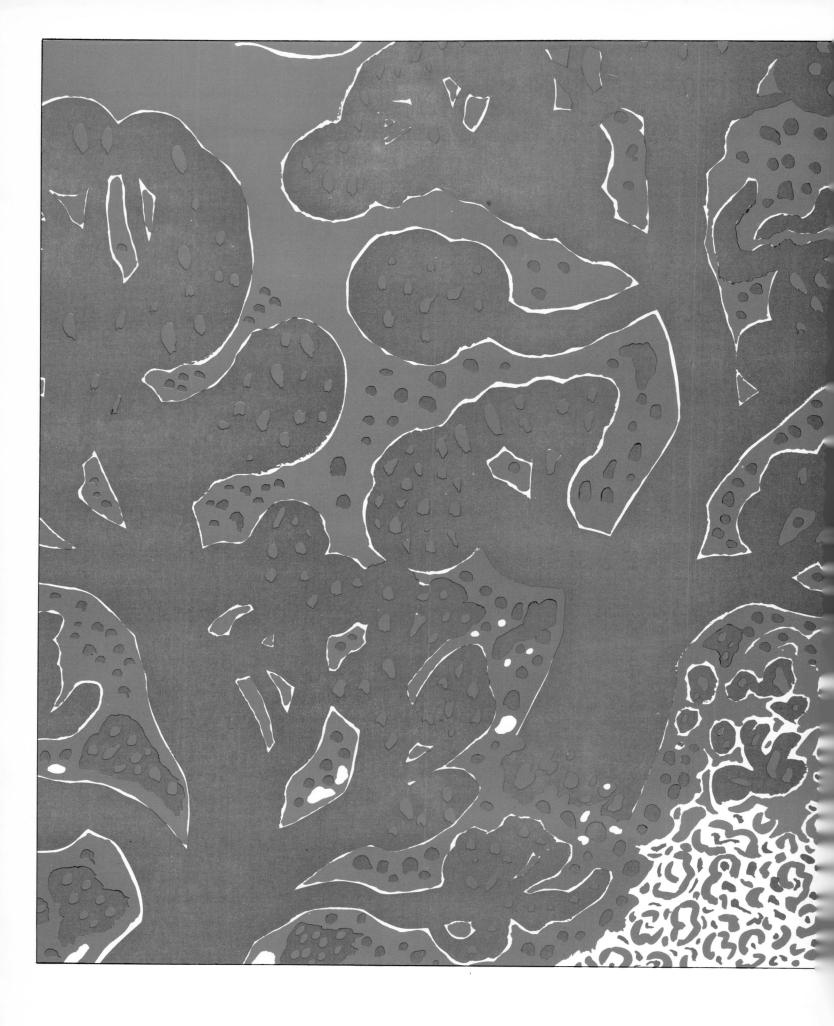

*Jean-Jacques Sempé/1974*

**PROGRESS**

*Edward Sorel/1976*

The caricaturist (to paraphrase Henri Bergson) who alters the size of a nose but respects nature's basic blueprint is as successful a sculptor as Nature herself. A sensitive use of exaggeration is the essence of his gift. Edward Sorel's cartoons are among the few that have this quality, while at the same time they are savage indictments of those being caricatured. During the mid-sixties and seventies, a period of social and political turmoil, Sorel unmasked those who perpetuated the Vietnam War, fostered the Watergate fiasco, and plunged the country into further amoral excesses. As few cartoonists are able to do in this day and age, he created images which spoke of the unarticulated feelings of a disillusioned generation. He did so with a sense of comic style that was as devastating as it was beguiling.

Sorel is a New Yorker. His earliest contact with art was "Dick Tracy." As a child he took art classes for poor kids at the Little Red Schoolhouse. At the age of ten he did "terrific stuff," which was hung at the Whitney Museum. He attended Cooper Union, where he was encouraged to let his drafting ability atrophy, and by the time he left—never having had a life class—he couldn't draw. He was fired from eleven advertising jobs—a record for a Cooper Union grad. "They thought I was incompetent, but liked me personally—a great source of comfort during those trying years." He and classmate Seymour Chwast decided that free-lance work was necessary, so they produced a promotion piece: "Everyone was doing blotters that year. We decided to do something different—'The Push Pin Almanac,' for which I take credit for the name. The response to this four-page mailer was terrific." They were soon encouraged to start a studio of their own, and Milton Glaser was invited in as a partner. By his own admission, Sorel's early work was inferior: "Working next to Sy and Milt, I had the temerity to work in line—unfortunately they were constipated parodies of eighteenth-century cross-hatchings." He left Push Pin, moved uptown, and became a designer. Soon he moved out of the city altogether. Happily, his new neighbor was illustrator R.A. Parker: "Parker did drawings without tracings (Push Pin was the master of the slip-sheet and light box). I began to draw direct and developed a personal voice for the first time." Since he has an obsession for detail and likeness, he found it hard to work in this manner. He uses scores of pads of cheap paper because it often takes dozens of starts before achieving success.

Sorel and Levine started caricaturing around 1965 at *Monocle:* "We both owe a great deal to Lyndon Johnson." Sorel came from a politically astute family and grew up during the thirties, a time of political ferment: "Instinctively, I knew government was the enemy." However, he never believed his drawings would significantly change policy: "The most I hoped for was that they would assure people who already held similar views. In fact, political cartoons are never very funny when you don't agree with them." He created his caustic "Bestiary" for *Ramparts* and "The Spokesman" for *Esquire.* King Features signed him to a weekly syndication: "By getting forty editors drunk, I was in forty newspapers that were a little to the left of Hermann Göring." He lost many of them when the editors began to question his patriotism. Although he did drawings for numerous publications, it was not until the *Village Voice* afforded him sinecure that he had a home for his criticism.

"All good humorists are basically teachers. If there is no point of view to be had, then we are decorators. My political cartoons are devoted to contradictions. I am not driven to comment about the starving masses. What concerns me are the liars that rule us. Most of my venom I reserve for so-called liberals—I've devoted more cartoon space to Humphrey and Javits; for me they are more hypocritical than Reagan, Ford, or Nixon." His drawings are studies of corruption and his comic movie posters have been a successful means of placing his targets in absurd, yet believable, situations. Sorel's ability to synthesize graphic elements from Rowlandson, Kley, Beerbohm, Gulbransson, and Auberbach-Levy strengthens his own comedies. His art is self-assured, but modesty sometimes overpowers him: "Once or twice I do something that is funny. I really don't know if it's good—the only clue I have is if I hope that it doesn't get lost before I deliver it."

**ANOTHER HOSTAGE SITUATION**

*Edward Sorel/1977*

**HENRY**

*Edward Sorel/1979*

**GODFATHER SAM**

*Edward Sorel/1978*

**EVOLUTION**
*Edward Sorel/1974*

**A QUESTION OF PRIORITIES**
*Edward Sorel/1978*

**THE GLUTTON**

*Edward Sorel/1977*

**JUBILEE POSTCARD**
*Ralph Steadman/1969*

# Ralph Steadman

The best cartoonists distill what they've derived from earlier generations into distinctive modes of personal expression. Ralph Steadman has applied a passion for the works of Grosz, Dix, and Searle in creating his own savagely critical cartoons. He has rejected the staid civility of modern British cartooning in favor of a German *Neue Sachlichkeit* grotesquery. But unlike the work of his Weimarian predecessors, whose harsh—sometimes pedantic—social commentaries often lacked a humorous cutting edge, Steadman's drawings are imbued with comic energy. He is an adept satiric journalist who creates visual essays that report on the absurdity of political life. The Watergate hearings, Republican and Democratic conventions, and the Patty Hearst trial, among others, are syntheses of broader human concerns which are so grand in scope that most satirists cannot approach them with personal commitment. Steadman attends these spectacles as a way to localize his commentaries. Usually the results are unbridled satires, rendered in a stark, albeit distorted, realism.

Steadman was born in Wallasey, Cheshire, England. His art education began with a "You Can Learn to Draw" matchbox advertisement. At East Ham Technical College he studied life drawing. He received further instruction at the London School of Printing and Graphic Arts, where he realized that there was more to drawing than just filling up space. His early attempts at cartooning were gags rendered in the benign styles of Giles and Hoffnung. Exposure to the German school, and a viewing of Luis Buñuel's film *L'Age d'Or*, changed his graphic emphasis. He submitted outrageous cartoons to *Punch* which were always rejected. The *Daily Telegraph* began to publish his caricatures on a regular basis, and he submitted drawings to the radical *Private Eye*. The "kink in his brain" was noticed across the ocean by editors at *Scanlan's* who brought him over to cover the Kentucky Derby with Hunter S. Thompson, an encounter which blossomed into an exciting marriage of words and pictures. Of Steadman, Thompson says: "[He] thinks more like a writer. . . . He comes to grips with a story sort of the same way

I do. . . . He doesn't merely render a scene, he interprets it."

Steadman is at the same time fascinated and repelled by America, and this has become a significant focus of his work: "I was culture-shocked by the screaming life style when I first came here." Although his travels to the New World are limited to once every few years, he is passionate about American political trends: "There is nothing going on in England. Americans have the government I love. It's amazing that there are so many venal characters in offices of respectability. It has become the norm, and people accept it as if they were schoolchildren overpowered by a sadistic schoolmaster. The current administration sets in motion a pattern of nostalgia that everybody there seems to want." He applies a no-holds-barred philosophy to caricature. He employs a sculptural sensibility in which he exaggerates the slightest physical flaw. He can metamorphose a molehill of a nose into Kilimanjaro—and often completes the character assassination with a few well-crafted words emanating in a speech balloon from the victim's own lips.

Steadman's approach is decidedly violent. The screaming, scraping, and scratching of his drawings call out for attention. "When Hunter was running for sheriff of Aspen, Colorado, he wanted me to do drawings of his opponents. He sent me photos of these gun-carrying rednecks. I definitely had a violent response to these people. I created horrid drawings with the caption 'Vote Before You See the Whites of Their Eyes.' I'm not the kind that would go out in the street and commit violence, so I do it in drawings. I find that this dynamic on the page doesn't hurt anyone in the long run." He realizes the need for choosing targets wisely. "There has to be total commitment. If you attack randomly, it's akin to harping and people get tired of it. But if you come back at odd times with strong critiques, you have greater effect." His intimate cartoon biography of Sigmund Freud was an exciting respite from the rigors of social comment. But the satiric instinct is always there: "When the Nixons of the world are in my sight, I get so excited I walk around the studio as if I was doing a war dance."

**ECOLOGY LESSON**

*Ralph Steadman/1971*

*Ralph Steadman/1971*

**ARCHITECTURAL FRANKENSTEIN**

*Ralph Steadman/1979*

**1984**
*Ralph Steadman/1974*

**STOP
THE BLOODY WHALING**
*Ralph Steadman/1979*

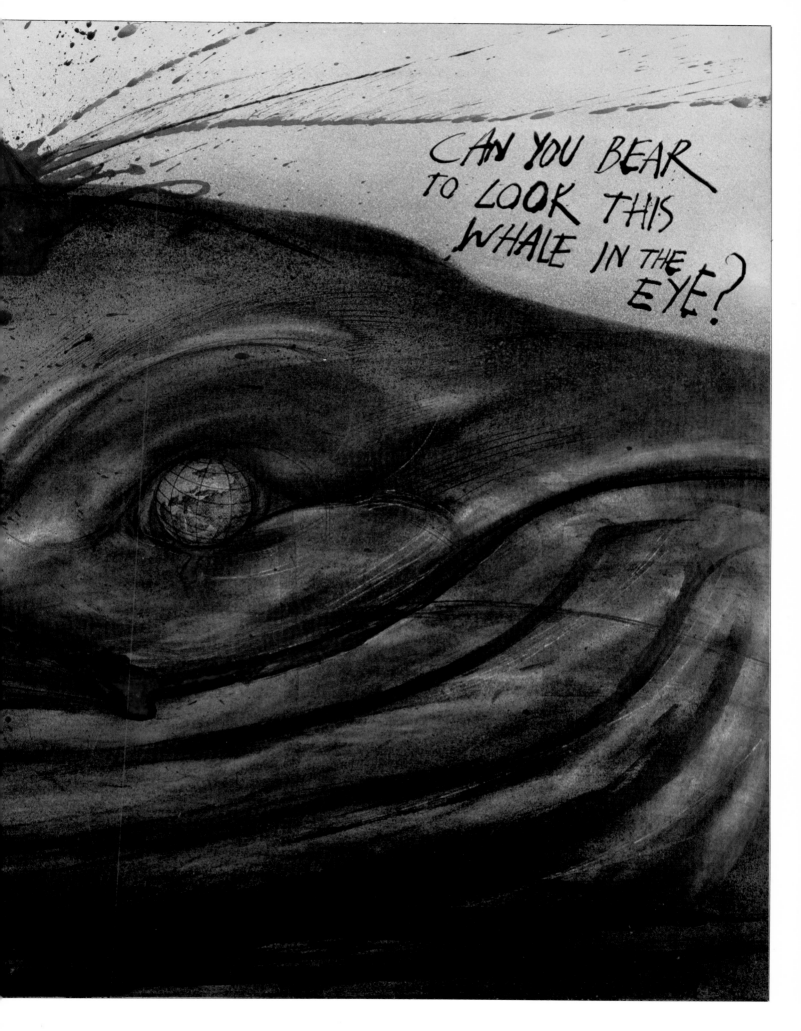

**SAVE THE SEALS**

*Ralph Steadman/1978*

*Ralph Steadman/1980*

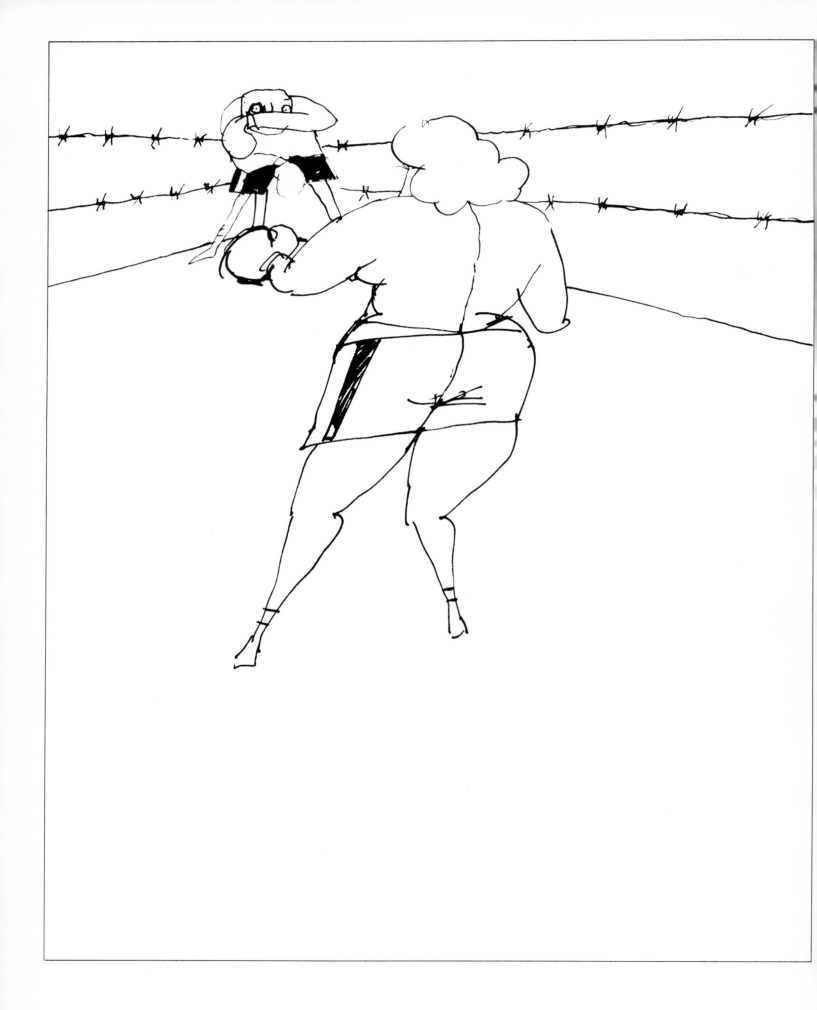

Tomi Ungerer/1964

# Tomi Ungerer

American cartoons are, for the most part, conservative. They are tastefully designed to entertain without causing unnecessary embarrassment to the viewer or host publication. Thankfully, from time to time, circumstance (aided by a courageous editor or art director) fosters the climate for a radical cartoonist to emerge—one who shocks the senses and at the same time redefines accepted norms. When Tomi Ungerer's work premiered during the mid-fifties, it was a graphic revelation—not simply because his powerful linear and color approach was in such contrast to the sentimental, lifeless forms of illustration being practiced, but because his satiric light exposed so many diabolical comedies in our collective unconscious. Writing in *Graphis,* Manuel Gasser said of Ungerer's audacity: "One cannot help noticing that [he] is a grown up child. Children have a habit of coming out with the truth, even when it is least opportune." It would be logical to assume that an artist with this explosive potential would have a limited cult following, but surprisingly, Ungerer became the *Wunderkind* of American graphic art (on his own terms). However, the methods of the commercial world eventually turned Ungerer's stomach, and in 1970 he broke the bonds. "My intentions were to get away from Madison Avenue and its gold-medal-sucking bogeymen. After thirteen years of hard work I had developed an allergy to the media."

Ungerer was born in Strasbourg, Alsace. He grew up under French rule and German occupation: "It left a strong imprint on me and gave me my first lesson in relativity and cynicism—the prison camps, the propaganda, the bombings...all this to culminate in an apotheosis of warfare....I must admit that to me as a child this was a big fun circus....My taste for the macabre certainly finds its roots here." He had no formal art training. He joined the Sahara camel corps and was discharged for ill health. At the age of twenty-four he moved to the United States and became a freelance illustrator. He did work for Henry Wolfe and Jerome Snyder, and produced countless children's books for Harper & Row and Diogenes. His most significant work in this area was *Crictor,* published in 1957. It was the first children's book to demolish convention by using a boa constrictor (then taboo) as its main character.

In the early years Ungerer had few outlets for his outrageous drawings, and so he prolifically filled innumerable books with remarkable conceptions (his *Underground Sketchbook* was famous years before publication). Now his satiric oeuvre is immense. His drawings—whether about sex, war, pain, death, or love—are all politically or socially motivated. His collection of drawings *America* is a chilling yet ironically sympathetic look at various loved and hated eccentricities of his second home. He rejects idealism, especially in terms of war—some wars are necessary evils, but Vietnam was stupid. His posters and drawings on this subject are savage indictments of that war's inhumanity and brutality. About this work he says: "America is a gutless country. I will do a political drawing because of a need I have. Out of anger." His pictures are historical essays dealing with mechanisms of life that ultimately wear out: "Everything I do has roots in Gibbons [*Decline and Fall of the Roman Empire*]. I am not really an artist, I am a thinker. I just use my drawings as a tool to make my thoughts accessible." Like Goya and Bosch, among his inspirations, who also dealt vividly with images of horror, Ungerer has a unique ability to translate these into understandable, often comic terms. Jonathan Miller describes Ungerer as illustrating "a world where things are coming apart....It is also a world in which men exploit each other like machines, in which men and women use each other as mechanical devices for their mutual satisfaction....In one sense the art of Tomi Ungerer is a derivative of sixty years of modern mechanized warfare. He is the artistic offspring of Passchendaele, Stalingrad, Auschwitz, and Algeria." Ungerer's current album, *Babylon,* is a revelation of our future in the manner of the prophet Daniel, who described the future to the King of Babylon—a collection of stark, lithographic images that will chill the bones of even the most cynical among us.

Ungerer now lives in County Cork, Ireland, where he is at work on a book of his surroundings. At age fifty, he is convinced that all he has done before is merely an apprenticeship for what is to follow.

Tomi Ungerer/1964

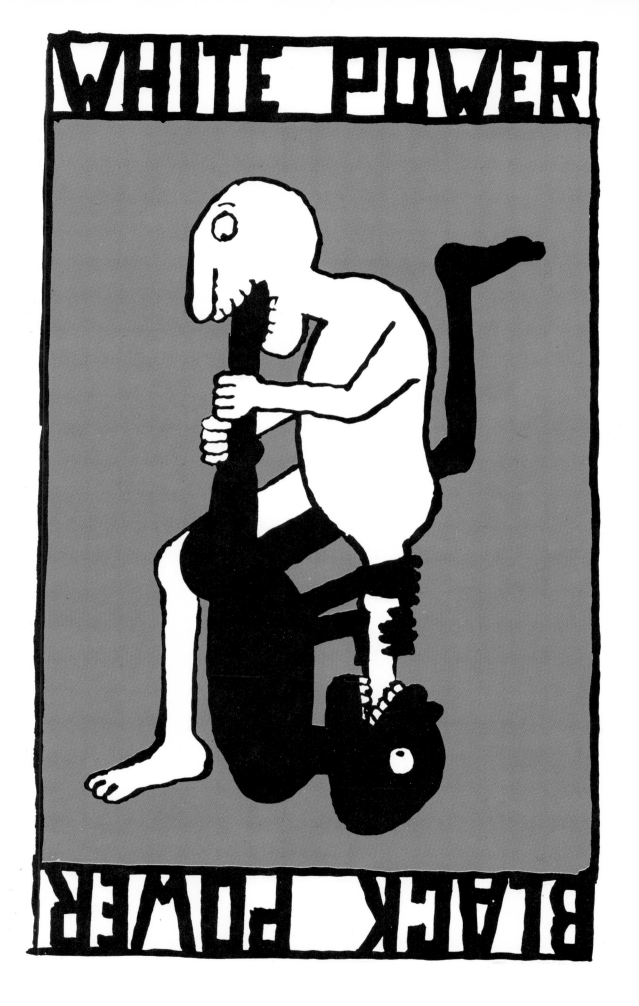

*Tomi Ungerer/1967*

*Tomi Ungerer/1972*

Tomi Ungerer/1978

*Tomi Ungerer/1978*

*Tomi Ungerer/1979*

"I'm sorry, Senator, it's some more of those crackpot conservationists."

*Gahan Wilson/1973*

# *Gahan Wilson*

**P**icture a dreary laboratory hidden deep within the bowels of an ancient university. Strewn among the skulls, the bats, the beakers of steaming liquid, and the jars of petrified goo are implements of the artist's trade—finely honed pencils, razor-sharp quills, and pads of ghost-white paper. In a tiny fluorescent-lit corner, hovering over the workbench, stands a tall, well-fed man with reddish-blond hair and moustache, wearing an ink-stained smock over his dapper, double-breasted blazer. He is mixing a wild concoction of ingredients into a black, paintlike brew. Wolfbane, dried blood, PCBs, a carcinogen or two, a strand of DNA, pages from Poe, Lovecraft, and Shelley, a drawing by Grosz, and the photos of senators, congressmen, and Ronald Reagan are all blended into a smooth purée. Without warning, he dips the tip of his finest nib and begins to draw an image that is at once horrendous, outrageous, and hysterically funny. Gahan Wilson is this mad cartoonist for whom the macabre—his leitmotiv—is always comic and the unthinkable is always on the horizon.

Wilson is a formidable satirist whose unique graphic niche is guarded by the diabolically innocent creatures he has invented to accentuate and exaggerate the human comedy. He is primarily known for his fascination with the weird and for his keen ability to make the distasteful positively joyful. However, he is also an adept commentator on the passing scene—particularly when it concerns matters of Armageddon. His bouts with social misanthropes and evil-doers are cleverly manifest in his single-panel horror shows. His monsters have dual roles: they are figments dredged from the depths of his imagination as well as metaphors for more general, all-encompassing concerns. He is delightful in his treatment of fifteen-legged spacelings and he is biting in his treatment of gnarled old statesmen and bug-eyed army officers.

Wilson was born in Evanston, Illinois, in 1930. He graduated from the Chicago Art Institute and then became an airman for a brief period. His early cartoon submissions met with rejection on the grounds that readers wouldn't understand them. Finally an art director at *Look* took a chance on Wilson and it proved to be successful. Wilson has been published in *The New York Times*, the *National Lampoon, The New Yorker* and other outlets, but *Playboy*, which affords him both freedom and popularity, is his foremost vehicle. His single-page color drawings always catch the viewer off guard—a brilliant marriage of logic and illogic is the keynote here. "Things must be logical in humor," he says; "if you don't have a convincing start, there is no possibility of establishing a joke. An example of this logic is what I do with werewolves—as far as I know it's exclusive to me. If you have a person who changes into a wolf, he'll be considerably reduced in size. His clothes won't fit him any longer, his shoes will fall off, and he will be weighed down by a sagging overcoat. So when I do werewolves, they are poor little hairy things floundering about." His Gothic sense derives from the movies and books he adores—Frankenstein, Dracula, and W.C. Fields are among his favorites. In a more serious arena, the dangers caused by modern technology, genetic engineering, and Dr. Strangeloves in general are in his sights. "It's ridiculous that businessmen in this country have been persistently trying to sell carcinogenic products, even when they have been outlawed. I find a perverse hilarity in this." Numerous drawings expose these sleeping monsters that we put in our stomachs and on our backs.

Wilson's marvelous juxtaposition of the absurd and the commonplace demands the viewer's attention. Ofttimes, however, his darkly shaded humor is merely the means of opening the eyes of his audience to a shocking revelation or human problem. A series of drawings, focusing on that insipid little yellow "smile face"—a popular novelty during the past several years—offers the occasion to lampoon the superficiality of trends.

Wilson is also an engaging storyteller, as evidenced in his ongoing comic strip for the *National Lampoon,* "Nuts." He thrives on the strictures of this format and allows his literary sensibility to take precedence. This is not the first venture in the strip medium, his syndicated Sunday panels exposed him to a much wider audience. Unlike "Nuts," which affords him creative freedom, he dropped the latter because "I was always censoring myself, worrying about what too many other people would think, rather than what I enjoy, results in bad cartooning."

"But surely it must have occurred to you that the wide differences in your backgrounds would make your marriage more than ordinarily difficult."

*Gahan Wilson/1970*

"Well, I guess that pretty well takes care of my anemia diagnosis."

*Gahan Wilson/1972*

"*Time and time again, I told it to him, over and over—DON'T SWIM IN THE LAKE!*"

*Gahan Wilson/1976*

*"Congratulations, Baer—I think you've wiped out the species!"*

*Gahan Wilson/1967*

**NUTS**

Remember how when you had all these great ideas to do things on your own? And then found your parents had you all planned up again?

Oh boy! School's out and I've got the whole summer to play in! And I won't have to study arithmetic for three months!

That evening...

I guess we might as well tell the kid, Madge—no point in holding back the good news!

You just wait until you hear what Daddy's done for you, dear!

It's costing me a lot of money, son, but we're going to send you to Camp Tall Lone Tree! Here's the folder.

The one Arthur Walsh went to last summer, remember?

He'll have a swell time, Madge, and it won't do him any harm if it gets a little rough in the woods.

I'll have to sew labels on every-thing, Harry! Art Walsh hated it!

SWIMMING HIKING BOATING ING ING ING

WELCOME TO CAMP TALL LONE TREE

I talked to the guy that runs it. Olaf Knudson. A real man, you know? He says if there's anything he hates worse than a sissy, it's a lazy kid!

He sounds nice, dear.

*Gahan Wilson/1975*

**NUTS**

REMEMBER WHEN YOU HAD BEEN EXPOSED TO THIS KID WITH THIS HORRIBLE DISEASE? ONE THAT PEOPLE COULD ACTUALLY DIE OF? ONE THAT COULD CRIPPLE YOU AND SCAR YOU? AND WAS VERY AWFUL AND REPULSIVE?

WELL, I COULD GET UP—THAT'S SOMETHING HERBIE MYERS COULDN'T GET DONE THE DAY HE CAUGHT IT. AND I DIDN'T THROW UP LAST NIGHT, AND NOTHING LEAKED ONTO THE PILLOW FROM MY EARS...

MY SHIT LOOKS ALRIGHT. BILL PEACH SHAT BLOOD AND GREEN STUFF WHEN HE GOT IT...

I ATE MY BREAKFAST WITHOUT PUKING, AND THE COLD AIR HASN'T MADE ME PASS OUT. MY FEET DIDN'T SWELL SO I COULDN'T PUT ON MY SHOES...

I HAVEN'T BROKEN OUT IN RED SPOTS LIKE THE BAKER KID DID BEFORE THEY SENT HIM TO THE HOSPITAL...

WHAT'S GOT YOU IN SUCH A GOOD MOOD?

NOTHING...

WHAT'S WRONG WITH HIS BEING IN A GOOD MOOD?

I'M ALIVE!!!!

I'M ALIVE!!!!

*Gahan Wilson*

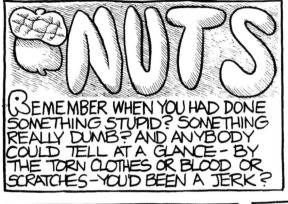

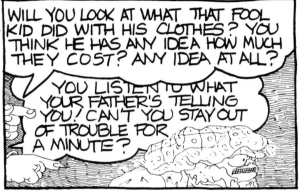

*Gahan Wilson/1975*

# SELECTED BIBLIOGRAPHY

**R.O. Blechman**
*The Juggler of Our Lady*
New York: Holt, 1953
*What a Funny Thing to Say*
(with Bernice K. Hunt)
New York: Dial Press, 1957
*R. O. Blechman: Behind the Lines*
New York: Hudson Hills Press, 1980

**George Booth**
*Dogs* (with Henry Morgan)
Boston: Houghton Mifflin, 1976
*Animals Animals Animals* (coeditor)
New York: Harper & Row, 1979
*Pussycats Need Love, Too*
New York: Dodd, Mead, 1980

**Jean-Pierre Desclozeaux**
*Nenesse et la marmelade d'oranges*
(with Picha, Puig Rosado, Sine)
Collection Parti-Pris
Paris: Calmann-Lévy, 1973
*130 dessins d'observation faits au Nouvel Observateur*
Grenoble: J. Glenat, 1974
*L'Oiseau-Moqueur*
Paris: Albin Michel, 1977

**Jules Feiffer**
*Sick, Sick, Sick*
New York: McGraw-Hill, 1956
*Passionella and Other Stories*
New York: McGraw-Hill, 1959
*Crawing Arnold*
New York: McGraw-Hill, 1959
*Feiffer's Album*
New York: Random House, 1963
*Harry, the Rat with Women: A Novel*
New York: McGraw-Hill, 1963
*Hold Me*
New York: Random House, 1963
*The Great Comic Book Heroes* (editor)
New York: Dial Press, 1965
*The Unexpurgated Memoirs of Bernard Mergendeiler*
New York: Random House, 1965
*Feiffer on Civil Rights*
New York: Anti-Defamation League of B'nai B'rith, 1966
*Little Murders*
New York: Random House, 1968
*Was Getekend, Feiffer*
Amsterdam: Meulenhoff, 1970

*The White House Murder Case: A Play in Two Acts* and *Dick and Jane: A One-Act Play*
New York: Grove Press, 1970
*Carnal Knowledge*
New York: Farrar, Straus & Giroux, 1971
*Pictures at a Prosecution: Drawings and Text from the Chicago Conspiracy Trial*
New York: Grove Press, 1971
*Knock, Knock*
New York: Hill & Wang, 1976
*Ackroyd*
New York: Simon & Schuster, 1977
*Tantrum*
New York: Alfred A. Knopf, 1979

**Paul Flora**
*Paul Flora*
Indianapolis: Bobbs-Merrill, 1959
*Paul Flora—Vamp Vivat*
Zurich: Diogenes, 1959
*Paul Flora*
Zurich: Diogenes, 1962
*Paul Flora: Der bürgerliche Wüstling*
Zurich: Diogenes, 1972
*Hungerburger Elegien: Zeichnungen 1943-1974*
Zurich: Diogenes, 1975
*Penthouse*
New York: Harry N. Abrams, 1979

**André François**
*L'Odyssée d'Ulysse*
Paris: Le Prat, 1947
*Lettres des Iles Baladar*
Paris: Gallimard, 1952
*The Tattooed Sailor and Other Cartoons from France*
New York: Alfred A. Knopf, 1953
*The Biting Eye of André François*
(Introduction by Ronald Searle)
London: Perpetua, 1960
*Santoun*
Paris: Editions Serg, 1972

**Edward Gorey**
*Case Record from a Sonnetrorium*
New York: Twayne Publishers, 1951
*Bleak House* (by Charles Dickens)
New York: Doubleday, 1953
*The Unstrung Harp or Mr. Earbrass Writes a Novel*
New York: Duell, Sloan & Pearce, 1953
*The Fatal Lozenge*
New York: Astor-Honor, 1960

*The Gashlycrumb Tinies or After the Outing*
New York: Simon & Schuster, 1963
*The Insect God*
New York: Simon & Schuster, 1963
*The West Wing*
New York: Simon & Schuster, 1963
*The Sinking Spell*
New York: Obolensky, 1965
*The Gilded Bat*
New York: Simon & Schuster, 1966
*The Monster Den or Look What Happened at My House—and to It*
Philadelphia: Lippincott, 1966
*The Doubtful Guest*
New York: Doubleday, 1967
*Fletcher and Zenobia* (with Victoria Chess)
New York: Hawthorn, 1967
*Utter Zoo*
New York: Hawthorn, 1967
*The Jumblies* (by Edward Lear)
New York: Young Scott Books, 1968
*Blue Aspic*
New York: Hawthorn, 1969
*Donald and the...*
Reading, Mass.: Addison-Wesley, 1969
*The Dong with a Luminous Nose* (by Edward Lear)
London: Chatto & Windus, 1969
*The Iron Tonic or A Winter Afternoon in Lonely Valley*
New York: Albondocani Press, 1969
*The Listing Attic* and *The Unstrung Harp*
London: Abelard, 1969
*At the Top of My Voice and Other Poems*
New York: W. W. Norton, 1970
*Penny Candy*
New York: Holt, Rinehart & Winston, 1970
*Someone Could Win a Polar Bear*
Philadelphia: Lippincott, 1970
*Fletcher and Zenobia Save the Circus*
New York: Dodd, Mead, 1971
*Sam and Emma*
New York: Parents Magazine Press, 1971
*The Shrinking of Treehorn*
New York: Holiday House, 1971
*The Sopping Thursday*
New York: Capra Press, 1971
*Story for Sarah: What Happened to a Little Girl*
New York: Albondocani Press, 1971
*Amphigorey*
New York: Putnam, 1972
*The Awdrey-Gore Legacy*
New York: Dodd, Mead, 1972

*Red Riding Hood*
New York: Atheneum, 1972
*The Black Doll: A Silent Film Script*
New York: Gotham Book Mart, 1973
*Categorey*
New York: Gotham Book Mart, 1973
*The Lavender Leotard or Going Alot to the New York City Ballet*
New York: Gotham Book Mart, 1973
*Amphigorey* (paper)
New York: Berkley Publishing, 1975
*Amphigorey Too*
New York: Putnam, 1975
*The Glorious Nosebleed*
New York: Dodd, Mead, 1975
*All Strange Away*
New York: Gotham Book Mart, 1976
*The Broken Spoke*
New York: Dodd, Mead, 1976
*Katz und Fuchs und Hund und Hummer*
Zurich: Diogenes, 1976
*Les passementeries horribles*
New York: Albondocani Press, 1976
*The Loathsome Couple*
New York: Dodd, Mead, 1977
*Gorey Endings*
New York: Workman, 1978
*Dracula: A Toy Theatre for All Ages*
New York: Scribners, 1979
*Gorey Games*
New York: Troubador, 1979

## Edward Koren
*Behind the Wheel*
New York: Holt, Rinehart & Winston, 1972
*Do You Want to Talk About It?*
New York: Pantheon, 1977
*Are You Happy? and Other Questions Lovers Ask*
New York: Pantheon, 1978
*So, There's Your Problem*
New York: Pantheon, 1980

## David Levine
*The Man from M.A.L.I.C.E.*
New York: E.P. Dutton, 1966
*Caricatures*
Paris: Stock, 1969
*Pens and Needles: Literary Caricatures*
Boston: Gambit, 1969
*No Known Survivors: David Levine's Political Plank*
Boston: Gambit, 1970
*The Fables of Aesop*
Boston: Gambit, 1975

*The Arts of David Levine*
New York: Alfred A. Knopf, 1978

## Bill Lee
*Absolutely No Persons Permitted*
*Beyond This Point* (coeditor)
New York: Dell, 1972
*OOPS*
New York: Dell, 1973
*The American Princess*
New York: Dell, 1974

## Pierre Le-Tan
*The Afternoon Cat*
New York: Pantheon, 1977
*Timothy's Dream Book*
New York: Farrar, Straus & Giroux, 1978
*Happy Birthday Oliver!*
New York: Random House, 1979

## Lou Myers
*Ha Ha Ha Hyenas*
New York: Coward McCann, 1971
*In Plenty of Time*
New York: Coward McCann, 1972
*Lou Myers: Absent and Accounted For*
New York: Workman, 1980

## Robert Osborn
*How to Ski*
New York: Coward McCann, 1942
*Dilbert, Just an Accident*
*Looking for a Place to Happen!*
New York: Coward McCann, 1943
*War Is No Damn Good!*
New York: Doubleday, 1946
*Low and Inside*
New York: Farrar, Straus & Young, 1953
*How to Shoot Pheasant*
New York: Coward McCann, 1955
*Osborn on Leisure*
New York: Simon & Schuster, 1957
*The Vulgarians*
Greenwich, Conn.: New York Graphic Society, 1960
*Dying to Smoke* (with Fred W. Benton)
Boston: Houghton Mifflin, 1964
*Missile Madness*
Boston: Houghton Mifflin, 1970
*Osborn Festival of Phobias*
New York: Liveright, 1971

## Hans Georg Rauch
*Rauchzeichen*
Geneva: Nebelspalter, 1969
*En Masse*
New York: Macmillan, 1975

*Battlelines*
New York: Scribners, 1977
*The Lines Are Coming: A Book About Drawing*
New York: Scribners, 1978

## Arnold Roth
*A Comick Book of Sports*
New York: Scribners, 1974
*A Comick Book of Pets*
New York: Scribners, 1976
*Two for Survival*
New York: Avon, 1979

## Ronald Searle
*Forty Drawings by Ronald Searle*
Cambridge: The University Press, 1946
*Le nouveau ballet anglais*
Paris: Montbrun, 1946
*Back to the Slaughterhouse and Other Ugly Moments*
London: MacDonald, 1953
*Whizz for Atoms: A Guide to Survival in the Twentieth Century for Fellow Pupils, Their Doting Maters, Pompous Paters, and Others Who Are Interested*
London: Parrish, 1956
*Paris Sketchbook*
London: Perpetua Books, 1957
*The Complete Molesworth*
London: Parrish, 1958
*The Dog's Ear Book*
New York: Thomas Y. Crowell, 1958
*The St. Trinian's Story: The Whole Ghastly Dossier Compiled by Kay Webb*
London: Perpetua Books, 1959
*Molesworth Back in the Jug Agane*
New York: Vanguard Press, 1960
*Refugees, 1960: A Report in Words and Drawings by Kay Webb & Ronald Searle*
Harmondsworth, Middlesex: Penguin Books, 1960
*Russia for Beginners*
London: Perpetua Books, 1960
*Escape from the Amazon*
London: Perpetua Books, 1964
*From Frozen North to Filthy Lucre* (with remarks by Groucho Marx)
New York: Viking Press, 1964
*Anatomie eines Adlers*
Munich: Desch, 1966
*Haven't We Met Before Somewhere?: Germany from the Inside Out* (with Heinz Huber)
New York: Viking Press, 1966

*The Square Egg*
London: Weidenfeld & Nicolson, 1968
*The Adventures of Baron Münchhausen*
New York: Pantheon, 1969
*The Great Fur Opera*
Toronto: McClelland & Stewart, 1970
*Secret Sketchbook: The Back Streets of Hamburg*
London: Weidenfeld & Nicolson, 1970
*Ronald Searle: Bibliothèque Nationale*
Paris: Bibliothèque Nationale, 1973
*La Caricature* (coeditor)
Geneva: Skira, 1974
*More Cats*
London: D. Dobson, 1975
*The Terror of St. Trinian's*
Hornchurch, Eng.: Ian Henry Publishers, 1976
*Paris, Paris* (by Irwin Shaw)
New York: Harcourt Brace Jovanovich, 1977
*Ronald Searle*
New York: Mayflower, 1979

## Jean-Jacques Sempé
*Women and Children First*
Brattleboro, Vt.: Stephen Greene Press, 1962
*Sauve qui peut*
Paris: Denoël, 1964
*Des hautes et des bas*
Paris: Denoël, 1970
*Face à face*
Paris: Denoël, 1972

*Bonjour, bonjour*
Paris: Denoël, 1974
*L'Ascension sociale de Monsieur Lambert*
Paris: Denoël, 1975
*The Musicians*
New York: Workman, 1980

## Edward Sorel
*King Carlo of Capri*
New York: Harcourt Brace, 1958
*The Duck in the Gun*
New York: Doubleday, 1969
*Magical Storybook*
New York: American Heritage Press, 1972
*Making the World Safe for Hypocrisy: A Collection of Satirical Drawings and Commentaries*
Chicago: Swallow Press, 1972
*Superpen: The Cartoons and Caricatures of Edward Sorel*
New York: Random House, 1979

## Ralph Steadman
*The Jelly Book*
New York: Scroll Press, 1970
*Dogs Bodies*
London: Transatlantic, 1971
*Lewis Carroll's Through the Looking Glass and What Alice Found There*
London: MacGibbon & Kee, 1972
*America*
New York: Random House, 1977

*Sigmund Freud*
New York: Paddington Press, 1979
*Sigmund Freud*
New York: Simon & Schuster, 1980

## Tomi Ungerer
*The Underground Sketch Book*
New York: Dover, 1973
*Tomi Ungerer's Compromises*
New York: Farrar, Straus & Giroux, 1970
*Fornicon*
Zurich: Diogenes, 1971
*The Poster Art of Tomi Ungerer*
New York: Darien House, 1971
*Abracadabra*
Cologne: Argos, 1979
*(More Ungerer books listed in Diogenes bibliography)*

## Gahan Wilson
*I Paint What I See*
New York: Simon & Schuster, 1971
*Playboy's Gahan Wilson*
Chicago: Playboy Press, 1973
*The Cracked Cosmos of Gahan Wilson*
New York: Grosset & Dunlap, 1975
*And Then We'll Get Him*
New York: Richard Marek, 1978
*Nuts*
New York: Richard Marek, 1978

# DIOGENES VERLAG CARTOON AND GRAPHICS BOOKS

### Paul Flora
*Der bürgerliche Wüstling*
*Die verwurzelten Tiroler und ihre bösen Feinde*
*Trauerflora*
*Veduten und Figuren*
*Der gebildete Gartenzwerg*
*Königsdramen*
*Hungerburger Elegien*

### Edward Gorey
*Das Vermächtnis der Miss D. Awdrey-Gore*
*The Vinegar Works*
*Die sehr gute Uhr*
*La Chauve-Souris Dorée*
*Das unglückselige Kind*
*An Ominous Gathering*

### Jean-Jacques Sempé
*Alles wird komplizierter*
*Monsieur Lambert*

*Von den Höhen und Tiefen*
*Carlino Caramel*
*St. Tropez*
*Nichts ist einfach*
*Bonjour, bonsoir*

### Tomi Ungerer
*The Party*
*Kompromisse*
*Fornicon*
*Weltschmerz*
*Basil Ratski*
*The Poster Art of Tomi Ungerer*
*America*
*Freut Euch des Lebens*
*Der Sexmaniak*
*Spiegelmensch*
*Der erfolgreiche Geschaftsmann*
*Adam & Eva*
*Babylon*